God's Little ...

pg 120
say ...

1-800-833-...

FAVOR IS THE WAY TO THE TOP °

INSIDE OF ME, IS THE SEED OF GREATNESS
FROM GOD

possessing
YOUR
healing

HEBREWS 2:9

ISAIAH 33:22

PSALM 113:7-9

JESUS WHAT IS YOUR WISDOM ABOUT
this

I CORIN 2

sleep - ELIJAH
8 MIRACLE OF ELIJAH

possessing
YOUR
healing

TAKING AUTHORITY OVER
SICKNESS IN YOUR LIFE

KYNAN T. BRIDGES

DESTINY IMAGE® PUBLISHERS, INC.
P.O. Box 310, Shippensburg, PA 17257-0310
"Promoting Inspired Lives."

This book and all other Destiny Image, Revival Press, MercyPlace, Fresh Bread, Destiny Image Fiction, and Treasure House books are available at Christian bookstores and distributors worldwide.

For a U.S. bookstore nearest you, call 1-800-722-6774.
For more information on foreign distributors, call 717-532-3040.
Reach us on the Internet: www.destinyimage.com.

ISBN 13 TP: 978-0-7684-4204-5
ISBN 13 Ebook: 978-0-7684-8743-5

For Worldwide Distribution, Printed in the U.S.A.
1 2 3 4 5 6 7 8 / 17 16 15 14 13

Dedication

I want to dedicate this book to the Lord Jesus Christ, the King of kings and Lord of lords. I also want to dedicate it to Gloria Bridges—my lovely and virtuous wife, the mother of my three beautiful children (Ella, Naomi, and Isaac), and my number-one supporter in life and ministry. To my church family who has been instrumental in praying for and supporting this project—God bless you!

Endorsements

If you are someone who has never considered that miraculous healing exists today, than reading this book may open your eyes to the reality of the supernatural.

HEIDI BAKER, PHD
Founding Director, Iris Global

In this dynamic book, *Possessing Your Healing*, the reader will discover the richness of the promises of God concerning healing, and the reality that healing is the "children's bread." Pastor Kynan has masterfully driven home the point that walking in divine health is a covenant right, and benefit of privilege to all believers mutually, and how walking in simple faith will cause the healing power of God to be made manifest in a life that is loaded with expectation.

DR. MARK T. JONES SR.
Manifestations Worldwide Inc.

God is still working miracles and healing the sick in this hour. Kynan Bridges has taken the time to invite you to embrace all that Christ's Finished Work has provided for you. His Word is a healing Word and His Presence indeed is Healing Presence. Embrace the truths enclosed in this volume and let God touch you in a significant way.

Dr. Mark J. Chironna
Church on the Living Edge
Mark Chironna Ministries

Pastor Kynan Bridges' book, *Possessing Your Healing*, shows that he has great insight into what the Believer must do to increase their level of faith for healing, and how to release their faith and possess their healing. I highly recommend that Christians make the small investment to purchase this book, read it, meditate on its principles and scriptures, and then reap the great dividends that it will produce in your life.

Dr. Douglas J. Wingate
President and Founder
Life Christian University

Contents

Preface

In more than fifteen years of being a believer, I have never been more convinced than I am now about the subject of divine healing. As soon as I received revelation of what God's Word had to say about the subject, my life was changed forever.

I realize that many people in the Body of Christ are living below what they have been given in Christ. I cannot imagine a world in which God only blessed us sometimes, or woke us up only on some mornings, or gave us only a portion of His blood. As ridiculous as these examples might sound, they are exactly what people assert when they say "God might heal."

The purpose of this book is to illuminate the minds of born-again believers and empower them to confidently appropriate every spiritual blessing they have been given in Christ.

This book will also provide a biblical foundation for divine healing that will strengthen your knowledge of what the Bible has to say about healing.

Lastly, this book will help increase your faith. Our ability to receive anything from God is contingent upon faith in His Word. As you read, my prayer is that the Holy Spirit will speak to your spirit and enable you to hear what the Word of God is saying to you today.

God bless!

CHAPTER 1

God's Original Design

In Genesis 1:26, God said the following:

> *Let us make man in our image, after our likeness: and let them have dominion over the fish of the sea, and over the fowl of the air, and over the cattle, and over all the earth, and over every creeping thing that creepeth upon the earth.*

The word translated "man" in this passage is the Hebrew masculine noun *adam* (Strong, H119).[1] Typically, this noun refers to humanity as a whole. In other words, God's original intent for His creation was for humankind to subdue the earth.

God wanted an earth populated with the men and women He created. The Hebrew words for "image" and "likeness" are the words *tselem* (Strong, H6754) and *demuwth* (Strong, H1823), which mean "resemblance" and "similitude," respectively. God wanted the men and women He created to not only take dominion over the earth, but also to look, function, and act like Him in every way.

This was God's original design: a perfect race of men and women who looked and acted exactly like God.

In Genesis 2:5, we are told that there was no one to till the ground. This is very interesting because, in Genesis 1:26, God said, "Let us make man...." Yet in Genesis 2:5, man was not yet formed. However, if you continue on to Genesis 2:7, you will see that God "formed man of the dust...and breathed into his nostrils..." so that man became a "living soul."

This is an amazing truth because it gives us great insight into the mind of God.

In Genesis 1:26, God made or created man, but in Genesis 2:7, God gave him form. The word translated "form" in Hebrew is the word *yatsar*, which means "to frame... pre-ordain," to give "divine activity" (Strong, H3335) and purpose.

In Genesis chapter 1 God created man as a spiritual being first. Then in Genesis chapter 2 He framed him and gave him purpose and divine activity. This is why humanity is in the state it is in; humans are spiritual beings, but when they lack divine activity and divine purpose, they cannot operate in the things of God.

Understanding divine purpose helps us see what God intended for us to have from the very beginning of creation. He wanted us to be perfect, to lack nothing, and to take dominion. Adam was never sick. He was never impoverished. There was not a time when he tried to speak to God and didn't get a response. He was in perfect communion and fellowship with God. He was in divine health.

Unfortunately, due to sin, this perfect relationship did not last. In Genesis chapter 3, Adam and Eve disobeyed God and ate of the tree of the knowledge of good and evil. This sin perverted humankind's relationship with a holy God, and ushered in a curse. Due to our tripartite nature, the curse of sin and disobedience affected every area of human existence: spirit, soul, and body.

God warned Adam that the day he ate of the tree of the knowledge of good and evil he would surely die (see Gen. 2:17). That is exactly what happened—in all three of the areas we are about to discuss.

SPIRITUAL DEATH

The most consequential aspect of this death was spiritual: humankind was separated from eternal fellowship with its Creator. The separation severed our access to eternal life with God and to spiritual authority in the earth. By virtue of Adam's transgression, humanity relinquished its God-given right to rule the earth. It instead transferred this right to Satan.

DEATH OF MIND, WILL, AND EMOTIONS

This is the death of the soul. When Adam sinned, he ushered in the sin consciousness. He hid from the presence of God due to the guilt of his transgression. For the first time in their existence, Adam and Eve became acquainted with fear.

Human decisions were affected by this sin. It caused us to have a natural inclination to rebel and walk in the carnal nature.

PHYSICAL DEATH

Through sin, Adam (and all humans) lost the physical capacity to live forever. Having been put out of the Garden of Eden, he became subject to the natural elements, which he had not previously been subject to. This meant that he could become sick or poor; he could suffer lack; and his organs would eventually fail, causing death.

God's original design included an eternal life of perfect righteousness and fellowship with Him, divine health, and spiritual and physical prosperity. God originally intended for the humans He created to possess both His attributes and His authority, which was to be exercised on the earth.

Sin is the force that separates man from God's original design. Jesus Christ came to destroy the works of Satan and bring man back to a place of eternal fellowship with God—in other words, to restore man back to perfection. As a matter of fact, born-again believers are made perfect in Christ: "And ye are complete in Him, which is the head of all principality and power..." (Col. 2:10).

Christ stands exalted forever at the right hand of the Father. This means that because we are in Christ, we stand perfectly complete and restored before the Father in heavenly places.

Christ redeemed us from Adam's curse when He died on the cross for our sins and took the penalty of death on our behalf. God's original design was fully restored to us; therefore, it is important to understand God's original design. Without understanding it, we cannot fully grasp what salvation was intended to produce in the life of a born-again believer.

In many sectors of Christianity, Jesus Christ is presented as a religious relic, an object of worship; but the biblical truth is that Christ is a living Redeemer who paid a tremendous price for our salvation. This salvation has profound implications for every New Covenant believer. The salvation that Christ accomplished not only impacts the total man, but it has afforded us eternal access to God's original design.

Divine healing is a huge part of this redemptive package. The more we understand God's original plan for us, the more conscious we are of what Christ accomplished on the cross—and the better positioned we are to place a demand on what He accomplished, *especially healing*.

POWER IN PRAYER

Father, thank You for the life You have prepared for me and for all Your children. I draw on Your Spirit and Your grace so that I might perceive my life, and the purpose of my life, through Your eyes. I set my heart in agreement with Your Word, so that I will enter into the fullness of Your redemptive plan. In Jesus' name. Amen.

ENDNOTE

1. All Strong's numbers marked with an "H" are from the "Hebrew and Aramaic Dictionary." Numbers marked with a "G" are from the "Greek Dictionary." See Bibliography for full publication details.

CHAPTER 2

What Is
Divine Healing?

In these pages, you will learn how to possess your healing—but before you learn that, you must understand what exactly divine healing is.

Simply put, divine healing is enjoyed when you and I apply the covenant promise of the Word of God to our physical bodies. When we became born again, we came under the authority and control of Jesus Christ. Our bodies became the temple of the Holy Spirit. God literally purchased us back from Satan. This purchase included every aspect of our being, including our physical bodies.

In First Corinthians 6:20, the Word tells us: "For ye are bought with a price: therefore glorify God in your body, and in your spirit, which are God's." Through the blood of Jesus Christ, God purchased the legal right to own our bodies. We belong to Him in every way.

GOD'S PRESENCE IN THE "TEMPLE"

When God comes to inhabit the temple called *the body*, He brings the fullness of His presence into our physical being, through the human spirit. This means that the Spirit that raised Jesus from the dead is the same Spirit that dwells within us. When the Spirit comes in, He quickens every cell in our bodies and brings our bodies under submission to the Lordship of Jesus Christ.

Because of the indwelling of God's Spirit within us, sickness has no place in us. Therefore, you and I no longer have the right to be sick! Our bodies don't belong to us anymore. We understand what the Bible says concerning our bodies being the temple of the Holy Spirit; we also know about the necessity to flee sexual sin. Yet many people don't realize that sickness and disease *don't belong* in the temple of the Holy Spirit, either.

Notice what the Bible says in First Corinthians 6:19:

> *What? know ye not that your body is the temple of the Holy Ghost which is in you, which ye have of God, and ye are not your own?*

The word translated "temple" is the Greek word *naos*, which means "...sacred edifice (or sanctuary)..." (Strong, G3485). The idea is that our bodies are the most sacred place there is as it relates to the habitation of the Spirit of God.

In the Old Testament, God dwelt only in the Holy of Holies, which was housed within the inner court of the Tabernacle. In the New Testament, He makes our spirit and physical body His sacred place.

This helps us to understand what divine healing is all about. The word *heal* means to cure or "to make sound or whole." Divine healing is the manifestation of this wholeness in our bodies. When we refer to the body, we include the mind as well. In the Gospel of Mark chapter 5, we see that Jesus healed a man possessed with several demons. After this encounter the Scripture records in verse 15 that he was "clothed, and in his right mind...."

It is wonderful to know that the healing power of Christ extends to every facet of our beings, even our minds. One of the reasons we include the mind is that sickness is not limited to the physical body. Sometimes people are afflicted in their minds, as in the case of the Gaderene demoniac.

Mental illness is common in the United States. I personally know many people who have had to battle depression, schizophrenia, bipolar disorder, and suicidal thoughts. And I personally know what it means to be restored spiritually, physically, and mentally. Unfortunately, the devil does not discriminate in the areas of his attack. Therefore, we assert that divine healing is the supernatural curing and restoration of the total person.

Even greater news: divine healing includes not only mental illness, but all human emotions. The Bible says:

> *To appoint unto them that mourn in Zion, to give into them beauty for ashes, the oil of joy for mourning, the garment of praise for the spirit of heaviness; that they may be called trees of righteousness, the planting of the LORD, that he might be glorified* (Isaiah 61:3).

We will spend much time on the physical manifestation of healing, focusing on anything that occurs anywhere in the body. Divine healing covers all of it.

A DIVINE RIGHT

Divine healing already belongs to born-again believers. It is our right! Think about what a right is: it denotes "a moral or legal entitlement to have or obtain something or to act in a certain way." The implications of something being our rights are very great. When you know that you have a legal right to something, it changes the level of boldness by which you act on it.

If a person were to impose on you in a physical way against your will, it would be called assault or molestation, because your personal space legally belongs to you. In the same manner, when Satan afflicts you with sickness and disease, he is imposing on space that does not belong to him. He is breaking the law. You have a legal right to resist him.

Some Christians would suggest that healing is something God "might do" if He feels like it. The problem with that way of thinking is that it does not line up with the Word of God. Healing is the divine right of every born-again believer. It is something that Jesus Christ purchased for us on the cross of Calvary, as First Peter 2:24 explains:

> *Who his own self bare our sins in his own body on the tree, that we, being dead to sins, should live unto righteousness: by whose stripes ye were healed.*

This is the authority on which a believer can receive and walk in divine healing.

THE "TOTAL" GOSPEL

Many people compartmentalize the Gospel. They treat the Bible like a buffet where they can pick and choose which blessings are relevant for today and which blessings are no longer appealing or convenient. If we do this, then we are telling God that His Word is not absolute. Ultimately, we are calling Him a liar.

Consider what Jesus said in the Gospel of Luke:

> *The Spirit of the Lord is upon me, because he hath anointed me to preach the gospel to the poor; he hath sent me **to heal the brokenhearted, to preach deliverance to the captives, and recovering of sight to the blind, to set at liberty them that are bruised,** to preach the acceptable year of the Lord* (Luke 4:18-19).

This is one of the most powerful statements in the Bible, because it sets forth God's sovereign plan for sending His Son to the earth. God's intent was and is to restore His children in every area of their lives.

Christ did not come solely so we could be forgiven of our sins. Nor did He come solely so we could be physically restored. He came so that we could be completely redeemed in every area. Christ's sacrifice has provided for us the legal grounds to walk in all of the promises and blessings of the Word of God, including healing.

The curse of Adam's sin affected us physically. Therefore, it is appropriate that the eternal salvation Christ obtained for us also affects us physically. If our salvation can only affect our spiritual being, then it is incomplete. Complete salvation involves spirit, soul, and body.

A few years ago, my wife, Gloria, experienced an irregular heartbeat. It started while she was pregnant with our second daughter, Naomi. When it first began, she was taken to the emergency room at the community hospital where she went through a series of tests. After hours of observation and a series of EKG and MRI tests produced no results, she was sent home with no specific diagnosis and no solution. Her ob-gyn decided that the irregular heartbeat was associated with the pregnancy, and dismissed the issue.

However, after weeks of complaining, my wife was referred to a cardiologist. Additional tests still produced no results. After our daughter was born, the condition continued to plague my wife and prevented her from completing the simplest of tasks without feeling sick. This became more serious than we had imagined.

At the time, we believed in divine healing but we were not as aggressive about it as we are today. The condition continued for about a year and a half. Finally we began to take authority over the situation, and my wife and I prayed for the issue to stop. One day while we were attending church services, the minister gave a word of knowledge and said, "Someone is being healed of an irregular heartbeat right now!"

Gloria immediately released her faith and received her healing. She never had an irregular heartbeat again.

The point of the illustration is to demonstrate that it does not matter what the illness or sickness is. Christ defeated it on the cross and has given you and me the legal right to receive healing. When we are fully convinced that healing is our right and not a privilege, then we will take authority over any symptom or sickness.

Matthew 8:16-17 says:

> *When the even was come, they brought unto him many that were possessed with devils: and he cast out the spirits with his word, and healed all that were sick: that it might be fulfilled which was spoken by Esaias the prophet, saying, **Himself took our infirmities, and bare our sicknesses.***

If Christ bore our sicknesses, we no longer need to bear them. Many well-intentioned and not so well-intentioned pastors are teaching people that Christ wants them to be comfortable in their sicknesses. That is a lie from the depths of Hades!

Christ came to provide healing and divine health in the atonement. Divine healing is what takes place when a born-again believer appropriates the Word of God in his or her "temple" and receives a manifestation of that Word, to the extent that it changes the state of the person's physical, mental, and emotional being.

When I was a young man growing up in Atlanta, Georgia, I remember going with my dad to dump scrap metal and other refuse in the waste yard. It was summertime, and I can remember the smell of decomposing trash. It was pretty horrible.

I want you to imagine for a moment someone taking the trash from the waste compound and dumping it in your backyard. It would be a serious problem. Why? Because that is where you live. That place is precious to you. Your children play in the backyard.

Now imagine for a moment that someone did the same thing in God's temple—literally taking trash and waste and spreading it across the altar. It's unimaginable! Yet, this is exactly what Satan does when he tries to afflict believers with sickness and disease.

Be encouraged: we have been given authority over Satan's attempts to "dump trash" in our bodies.

POWER IN PRAYER

Father, in the name of Jesus Christ, I come to You now with confidence in Your Word. I thank You that I have a revelation of divine healing in my heart. I believe that healing is Your will for my life. I take authority over every lie of Satan that says You will not heal me. I take authority over a religious spirit that says healing is not for everyone. Healing is for me! I walk in the benefits of Calvary right now. In Jesus' name. Amen.

CHAPTER 3

Healing and the Atonement

And not only so, but we also joy in God through our Lord Jesus Christ, by whom we have now received the atonement....For if by one man's offence death reigned by one; much more they which receive abundance of grace and of the gift of righteousness shall reign in life by one, Jesus Christ (Romans 5:11,17).

The word for "atonement" in the Greek is *katallage*. It means "exchange" or "restoration to (the divine) favor..." (Strong, G2643). The word suggests a transaction. In other words, an exchange took place on the cross of Calvary. Christ took on our sin so that we could take on His righteousness.

The implication of this exchange is much greater than we can imagine. He literally took our sickness so that we would be able to walk in His divine health.

Romans 5:17 tells us that, although death reigned by Adam's offense, those who receive "abundance of grace" and the "gift of righteousness shall reign in life...."

Earlier we established that the death ushered in through Adam's transgression affected humankind in three areas: spirit, soul, and body. Sin did not just affect us a little bit; it caused death to reign over us. Sin completely dominated our lives, and it still dominates the lives of those who are not in Christ.

In order for the atonement to be complete it would have to provide the polar opposite of what sin produced. It would not be enough for the atonement to stop the reign of death in our lives (spirit, soul, and body); it would also have to produce the ability to reign in life (spirit, soul, and body).

IMPLICATIONS OF RIGHTEOUSNESS

This is exactly what Jesus did on the cross. He restored us to a place of divine favor. This favor allows us to receive the gift of righteousness.

Many people do not understand the implications of righteousness. It is more than a moral transformation. Righteousness literally means being the way you were created to be, in a condition that is acceptable to God.

If you put righteousness in this context, it means that, through the cross, Jesus restored us to the way we ought to be. We were made acceptable to God through the blood of Christ. Our spiritual man was not the only part of us that was made the way it ought to be. The same is true of our bodies and minds.

When we *realize* that we were made the way we ought to be through Christ, then we can *reign* in life. God wants us to reign! He does not want us to merely get by on a wing and a prayer.

Too many believers are ignorant of what has been accomplished for them through the atonement. Notice what Romans 5:11 says: "*...by whom we have now **received** the atonement.*" The atonement has already been made on our behalf in the person of Jesus Christ. Yet the apostle Paul used the word *receive* to describe a believer's relationship to the atonement. We see the same word used in Romans 5:17, which says: "*they which **receive** abundance of grace and of the gift of righteousness....*"

The grace of God has been supplied in Christ, but in order to benefit from that grace we must *receive* it. What does it mean to receive? The word for "receive" in both verses is the Greek word *lambano*, which means "to take hold of...take possession of...*to take a thing due* (Strong, G2983).

This is the beauty of the cross: Christ has already done His part. The question is whether you and I will take possession of what He has already done. When we became born again, we received the right to approach God and enter into His presence without guilt or shame. We also received the right to walk in divine healing—with the same level of confidence and authority we have in the truth that our sins are atoned for.

The God who atoned for your sins is the same God who healed your body. The grace available to receive forgiveness is the same grace available to receive healing. The

problem is that many people have never received the atonement. They still live under the condemnation and guilt of
sin. As a result, they find it extremely difficult to receive
their healing.

When we realize that we are able to approach God
because of what Christ did, then we have a supernatural
boldness based on the strength of God's character.

The second aspect of the atonement is the reality that,
if Jesus is truly Lord over our life, then God's wrath has
been turned away from us forever. This is an aspect that
the Church has not truly grasped. Christ was and is our
propitiatory sacrifice. This means that the righteous wrath
of God toward us has been satisfied in the body and blood
of Christ, once and for all.

GOD IS NO LONGER ANGRY

Because of what Christ did, God is no longer seeking to
punish or destroy you. This truth is foundational to the Christian experience. But because of religion and false teaching in
the Church, believers still live as though God is about to
squish them with His heavenly "sin swatter." This is a wrong
perception of who God is. We must have a New Covenant
paradigm if we are to experience New Covenant promises.

Some would say, "But God does punish sin!"

Well, yes, He does. But there is a difference between
a born-again believer being subject to the spiritual law of
sowing and reaping, and a sinner being under the wrath
of God. The latter person's sins are subject to eternal
judgment, because the sacrifice of Calvary has not been

accepted. The born-again person has accepted the finished work of the cross. Therefore, the believer's sins have already been punished, in Christ.

HE TOOK OUR PLACE

Christ stood in the place of believers and received the wrath of God on their behalf. As a result, God can pour out His favor on believers as they stand in the place of Christ.

He stood in our place so that we could stand in His place. He became a curse, so that we could be made righteous. He was punished so that we could be rewarded. God's relationship with us is based on this positional reality: we have been placed in Christ, which is the most favorable position there is.

Many believers do not understand this biblical truth. As a result, they find themselves double-minded and frustrated. They vacillate back and forth between being saints and being sinners. It is a sort of bipolar relationship that they have with themselves.

My friend, it is absolute torment to live that way. If you are not certain about your salvation, then you need to be born again so that you can be sure of your relationship with God.

WE ARE NO LONGER SERVANTS

If you are born again and you are sure of it, then you need to be confident of this fact: God is not sitting on a stool in heaven waiting to send you to the devil's hell. As far as He is concerned, you and He are all right! As a matter of fact, He calls you His friend:

*Henceforth I call you not servants; for the servant knoweth not what his lord doeth: but I have called you **friends**; for all things that I have heard of my Father I have made known unto you* (John 15:15).

The blessing of Abraham that was imputed to us in Christ makes us friends of God:

And the scripture was fulfilled which saith, Abraham believed God, and it was imputed unto him for righteousness: and he was called the Friend of God (James 2:23).

Satan does not want those of us in the Body of Christ to know what God says about us. The devil wants us to remain in the dark about these truths so that he can continue to torment us. The time has come for us as God's people to take the promises of God's Word and apply them to our lives.

POWER IN PRAYER

Father, I thank You for Jesus Christ's atoning work on the cross of Calvary. I thank You that, through His finished work, I have been restored to perfect fellowship and communion with You. Right now I receive the fullness of the atonement in every area of my life. I thank You that I have the right to appropriate every covenant promise in your Word, based on the sacrifice of Jesus Christ. I renew my mind so that it is conformed to the truth of Your Word. I am 100 percent whole and restored through Jesus. In His name. Amen.

CHAPTER 4

God, the Healer

And said, If thou wilt diligently hearken to the voice of the Lord thy God, and wilt do that which is right in his sight, and wilt give ear to his commandments, and keep all his statutes, I will put none of these diseases upon thee, which I have brought upon the Egyptians: for I am the Lord that healeth thee (Exodus 15:26).

As stated already, everything we are able to receive from God is based upon our knowledge of who He is; and everything we know about God is based on the truth of His Word.

In the Old Testament, God revealed Himself to the children of Israel as the Healer. This revelation of His character was given along with a reference to the Ten Commandments: the promise of healing was attached to the commission to keep those commandments. In other words, God said, "I am the Lord your Healer. In order to experience this dimension of who I am, you need to align yourself with My Word."

The Hebrew word translated "Lord" in Exodus 15:26 is the word *Yehovah* (or *Jehovah*) which means "the existing One" (Strong, H3068). The word referring to God as Healer is the Hebrew word *rapha* which means "healer," or "physician" (Strong, H7495).

So we see that God (the only existing one) is the Healer. Healing is not just what He does; it is who He is. God is *Jehovah Rapha*. Healing is inseparable from His very nature. In order for God to be true to Himself, He has to heal. So there is no question as to whether or not it is God's will to heal. Does a doctor write prescriptions? Does a singer sing?

The nature of a person governs how he or she functions. God's nature is to heal.

MISCHARACTERIZING GOD

God is the Healer; this is part of the nature that governs Him. Healing is the natural manifestation of who He is. The "issue" of whether or not He heals is *not* an issue with God. Exodus 15:26 says, "If thou wilt diligently hearken to the voice of the LORD thy God...." In other words, God told the children of Israel they had a part: to align themselves with His Word, and to regard it.

The problem was that they were in the flesh and incapable of keeping His statutes, so they could not receive the fullness of God's promises in their lives. God tried to reveal Himself to the children of Israel, but they could not see

Him. They were so focused on their wilderness that they fell into the trap of mischaracterizing Him. They mistook their wilderness journey for punishment from God.

There is a similar attitude in the Body of Christ today. People are so preoccupied with their suffering that they fail to recognize that God is the Healer. We can never receive from someone we have judged or mischaracterized. God cannot be the one inflicting sickness on us and the one healing us at the same time. That is absolute insanity!

The Israelites coming out of Egypt were not born again; they did not have the Holy Ghost living inside them. Yet God still held them accountable. He held them so accountable that the majority of them died in the wilderness, never receiving His promise in their lives.

If God held them accountable, how much more are we saved people held accountable to appropriate God's Word in our lives?

By His Book

Every time you and I interact with God the Father, it must be on the basis of His Word. Many believers today base their relationship with God on their own feelings and emotions. The nature and character of God are consistent, regardless of how or what we feel. God's nature has nothing to do with the circumstances we find ourselves in; God remains the same regardless of our circumstances.

Whenever we attribute to God things that are opposite to His true nature, we set ourselves up for frustration. For example: A Christian man is diagnosed with terminal cancer, and someone tells him that the horrible disease is God's effort to teach him a lesson. If he buys into that lie and begins to see God as the one responsible for the sickness, he will tolerate it. After all, he believes *it is from God;* therefore, it must be God's will, right?

Wrong!

God has only one will: His Word. God relates to us based on His Word, not based on how we feel. So if we don't know who He is, we will hold Him responsible for things that have nothing to do with Him. We can never receive our healing from God if we are convinced that He is the one making us sick. Have you ever tried to receive something good from someone who continually hurts you? It is very difficult.

Imagine a bully at a school taking a kid's lunch one day and then paying for the kid's lunch the next day. What if this continued every day for six months? Would that make sense? Or imagine a burglar breaking into your home and stealing your property at gunpoint, then changing into a police uniform and responding to your 911 call.

Such inconsistency is both frustrating and confusing.

THE GREAT PHYSICIAN

Our faith can only operate where the will of God is known. If we are ignorant of who He is, we will also be ignorant of His will. As a result, we become incapable of receiving from Him. We must have a revelation of God, the Healer who heals all of our diseases. He is our Great Physician.

What if you went to the doctor and he or she intentionally prescribed harmful medicine that made you sick? How would you handle the situation? Not only would you find another doctor, but you would probably file a malpractice suit! Why? Because, what the doctor did is illegal. Doctors take oaths to always do their best to improve their patients' condition. They are not supposed to make sure their patients get sicker.

If such a scenario doesn't make sense in the natural realm, how could it make sense in the spiritual realm? We would never tolerate such contradictions from our earthly physicians. Why then should we expect them from our heavenly Father?

If God is the one who makes born-again believers sick, then He is not a physician at all.

THERE IS NO EXCUSE

Oftentimes, religious people make excuses for what they cannot explain. They cannot explain why they are being afflicted, so they pray, "Lord if it be Thy will...."

Here is what the Bible says: "...For this purpose the Son of God was manifested, that he might destroy the works of the devil" (1 John 3:8). Would God send His own Son to die on the cross, destroy the works of the devil (Satan), and rise from the dead, just so He could heap more works of the evil one upon us? Sickness is the work of the devil, not God. Christ was manifested to destroy the power of sickness in our lives, not to make us sick.

Genesis chapter 3 tells us that the serpent seduced Eve into rebelling against God. It was not God who seduced Eve into sin. Therefore, Satan was the party responsible for introducing humanity to the curse. Jesus Christ came to reverse the curse and restore to the Church the believers' right to walk in the fullness of His blessing. This is a very simple truth. Something this simple is often convoluted by religion and tradition.

A LACK OF KNOWLEDGE

We have to break free of our false perceptions of who God is. Until we adopt the biblical perception of God, we will find ourselves being victimized by Satan.

God longs to manifest Himself to His sons and daughters; but many have been ignorant of this truth. Ignorance is dangerous. As a matter of fact, the Bible says it is potentially deadly:

> *My people are destroyed for lack of knowledge: because thou hast rejected knowledge, I will also reject thee, that thou shalt be no priest to me: seeing thou hast forgotten the law of thy God, I will also forget thy children* (Hosea 4:6).

Notice that Hosea said, "my people are destroyed." God's people can be destroyed by what they do not know. The people spoken of in this passage were not pagan people; they were God's people.

The word translated "destroyed" means "to cease," or "to be cut off" (Strong, H1820). The word for "knowledge" is *da'ath,* indicating "discernment" or "perception" (Strong, H1847). The Hebrew word translated "for lack of" is *beliy.* It is an adverb of negation that signifies "without, no, not" (Strong, H1097). Together, the words literally convey a lack of discernment or perception.

This passage is saying that God's covenant people are cut off from the covenant (unable to receive its benefits) because of their lack of discernment or perception. God was not punishing them; they ceased to walk in the covenant promises due to their ignorance.

God also says they "rejected knowledge." In the original Hebrew, the word for "reject" is *ma'ac,* which means to "refuse" or "despise" (Strong, H3988). Not only were they ignorant of God's will, but they refused and despised it. They said "no" to God's promises and blessings for their lives.

Isn't that what some people do today? Not only are they not walking in divine healing, but they are actively resisting the message of healing.

THE ATTACK ON HEALING

There are people in the Church today who are attacking the biblical message of healing and divine health. They do not believe it is God's will to heal, and they substantiate their belief by pointing to the large number of Christians who are sick.

If I told you that because I have never been to the moon, the moon does not exist; or if I said that obtaining a perfect score on an exam was impossible because

I have never obtained a perfect score, would my assertions make sense to you? Yet, this illogical resistance to the Word of God (which is based on the defeat evident in certain believers' lives) is exactly what is happening in the Church today.

The Bible calls this attitude, "rejecting knowledge."

Not only are many people ignorant of what the Word of God says, they war against it in their hearts. Believers are fighting with all of their might for the right to be sick. Often, the same people insist that the gifts of the Spirit are no longer in operation. I ask them: "When did the gifts go out of business?"

It is deadly for us to have belief systems that are contrary to the Word of God. As we have said already: Everything about our ability to receive the blessings of God is contingent upon faith in the Word of God. That faith is based on the truth of God's Word. The truth is that God is the Healer.

IGNORANCE IS SATAN'S DESIRE

Satan wants the Church to be steeped in ignorance so he can continue to take advantage of believers. The enemy wants people to reject what God has for them on the basis of what they have been told.

Jesus asked in Mark 3:23, "How can Satan cast out Satan?" This is a profound question. Jesus challenged the accusation that He healed people through demonic power. In other words, how can someone who wants you to be sick turn around and heal you? That would divide Satan's purpose and his kingdom.

Terrorists don't rescue hostages. Doing so would defeat their purpose. Likewise, God cannot work against Himself. He cannot make people sick and simultaneously send Jesus to heal them.

The Israelites had the same problem in Christ's day that they had during the time of the prophet, Hosea. They mischaracterized God. They thought they knew Him; but in fact they did not. They could not recognize that Christ had been sent to be their Healer and Deliverer. As a result of wrong perceptions of the religious leaders of that day, many did not receive the fullness of what Christ had to offer.

If Satan can convince the Church that healing is an evil thing, they will never embrace it and never walk in it. As a matter of fact, they will work in concert with the devil to ensure that they never get healed.

The issue is one of godly discernment.

What if people discerned the truth and contended for divine healing with the same intensity as they contend for their right to be sick? Hospitals would be put out of business!

When we discern what the Word of God has made available to us, we will have strategic advantage over the enemy, every time. The reason I am so convinced about divine healing is because God is convinced about it. Walking in divine health is not a matter of human effort and ability; it is simply a matter of coming into agreement with what God's Word says.

THREE ASPECTS OF HEALING

There are three significant areas concerning healing that Jesus demonstrated throughout the Gospels: the power to heal, the will to heal, and the source of healing.

In Luke chapter 3, Jesus was baptized by John the Baptist. Immediately, Jesus received the Holy Spirit upon Him, and God announced from heaven: "Thou [Jesus] art my beloved Son; in thee I am well pleased" (Luke 3:22).

After He was baptized, Jesus was led into the Perean wilderness to be tempted of Satan. Following this victorious encounter, Jesus entered the synagogue on the Sabbath day and read from Isaiah 61. (See Luke 4.)

The reading of the scroll was a defining moment in Jesus' life and ministry. Every Jewish person in the community was familiar with Isaiah 61 because it dealt with the coming Messiah. In reading it, Jesus manifested His identity and the purpose of His public ministry. He not only showed Himself to be the Savior of Israel, but the Healer of Israel and all of God's people.

THE HEALING POWER OF THE CHRIST

In Luke 4:39, Jesus demonstrated His power to heal when He rebuked the fever afflicting Peter's mother-in-law. The Bible says that when He stood over her, He rebuked the fever and immediately the fever left her and she arose and ministered to them.

In Luke 4:43, Jesus informed the people that He had to preach the Kingdom of God to other cities also. Therefore, we see that the healing of Peter's mother-in-law was not an arbitrary event, but a manifestation of God's Kingdom. Jesus revealed to the people that He had the power to heal. There is no sickness that His healing power cannot overcome, no matter how severe or debilitating the ailment might be. Gospel accounts consistently reveal Jesus as the Healer who is always able to carry out the healing agenda of the Kingdom.

In Luke 5, Jesus further demonstrated the power to heal. The Bible clearly states that His power was "present to heal" (Luke 5:17). In that atmosphere, Jesus began to manifest His healing works in the lives of the people.

It is clear from this verse that Jesus is always in the healing business. The only requirement necessary to release His healing power is to have faith in it. When the people grabbed hold of this revelation, they began to take advantage of the atmosphere; they received their healings by faith.

The word for "power" in Luke 5:17 is the Greek word *dynamis* (or *dunamis*), which means "ability" (Strong, G1411). In essence, it is the idea of power in action. So the power of God was being put into action through the manifestation of healing. In other words, the power of God was being demonstrated through healing.

Two Greek words are primarily translated "power" in the Gospels: The first one is *dunamis*, as we have seen. The second is *exousia* (Strong, G1849). The latter deals with the right to do something, more specifically the legal right or authority. Not only did Jesus have the right to heal, but He had the power to heal.

A great analogy to illustrate these two meanings involves people in law enforcement. Their training, certification, and badges give them the legal right to pursue criminals. But their weapons provide the power to carry out this right. In the same way, Jesus had the authority to heal, but He demonstrated the power to heal by healing everyone who came into contact with Him.

THE HEALING WILL OF CHRIST

Not only did Jesus consistently demonstrate the power to heal, but He also demonstrated the *will* to heal. This is an important topic, especially in light of the modern idea that that "God will heal *if* it is His will."

In the fifth chapter of the Gospel of Luke, Jesus met a man who had leprosy, a very serious condition affecting a person's skin and nerve endings. It was not uncommon for those with leprosy to be missing limbs. Not only were lepers physically incapacitated, but they were also socially disenfranchised.

Yet Jesus had a close encounter with this leprous man. Instead of announcing to Jesus that he was unclean and that Jesus should not touch him (as the law required), the man fell on his face and said: "Lord, if thou wilt, thou canst make me clean" (Luke 5:12).

For this leper, it was not a matter of Jesus' *ability* to heal, but of His *willingness* to heal. In the next verse, Jesus answered, saying, "I will: be thou clean."

It is evident that Jesus not only has the power to heal, but is absolutely willing to heal.

Interestingly; the word for will in this passage is the Greek word *thelema* (Strong, G2307), which means "that which is willed, or gracious design." Jesus indicated to the leper that it was God's gracious design to heal him.

This provides great insight into the mind of God concerning healing. It reveals that Jesus carried out the will of God the Father by healing those who came into contact with Him. It is also important to note that the leper was the most unlikely person to receive this sort of miracle. In society of that time, leprosy was the most alienating condition a person could have; yet Jesus revealed His unconditional will and desire to heal it.

It is God's gracious plan to manifest healing in the lives of His people. Unless the people of God realize that it is God's will to heal them, they will simply accept sickness. They will see it as something God allows at times to teach His children a lesson.

This could not be further from the truth.

There is not a single instance recorded in any of the four Gospels in which Jesus refused to heal someone because it was God's will for the person to be sick. He never said that people should just be thankful to be alive, never complaining about their conditions. To even think such a thing is absurd. The Bible record is clear and consistent: Jesus' will is to heal people.

THE SOURCE OF HEALING

One of the most interesting aspects of the subject of healing is the source of healing. It is very clear to us that

Jesus has the power to heal. And we have seen that He possesses the unconditional will to heal. But what is the source of healing revealed through the Gospels?

One of the greatest misconceptions in the modern Church is that the healings Jesus performed in the Bible were due to His nature as the Son of God. Unfortunately, this line of thinking is the result of poor exegesis of scripture.

In Luke 4, Jesus announced in the synagogue that the Spirit of the Lord was upon Him (see Luke 4:18). This was a Messianic prophecy from Isaiah 61. It foretold the coming Jewish Messiah who would manifest the Kingdom of Yahweh.

By quoting from the Prophets in this way, Jesus made a very bold statement. Not only did He claim to be the Meshiach (Messiah), but He also proclaimed that He had the anointing of God. This anointing resulted from the Spirit of God being upon Him.

Jesus was the Son of Man anointed by Jehovah to fulfill a ministry on Earth. The word for "anointed" in this passage is the word *chrio* (Strong, G5548), which means to "anoint" or "consecrate for to an office or religious service." The word for "Anointed One" is *Christos* which literally means "the Anointed of God." This is where we derive the English word *Christ*.

Literally, Jesus was anointed by God. The anointing of the Holy Spirit was the source of His healing power. This is why it says in Luke 5:17 that "the power of the Lord was present to heal." This refers to the healing anointing of the

Spirit of God. It was through the Spirit of God that Jesus manifested healing in the lives of those who approached Him by faith.

Many people have a wrong understanding of the source of healing. Some believe that healing is a spontaneous act of grace or God's mercy. Some also suggest that, because Jesus was God in the flesh, the miraculous works He performed were exclusive to Him. But the Bible clearly shows the true source of divine healing to be the anointing of the Holy Spirit. God anointed and empowered Jesus to do the work necessary to manifest the Kingdom of God.

In John 5:19, Jesus declared that He could do nothing but that which He saw the Father doing. This statement provides even greater insight into the source of healing. Jesus explained that the only reason He was able to do these things (healing, etc.) was because of the presence of the Father.

Jesus received the anointing of the Holy Spirit after His baptism in Luke 3, which enabled Him to heal the sick and perform wondrous miracles. Jesus always remained in intimate fellowship with the Father. He always tapped into the source of power, and drew from that source what was necessary to demonstrate the Kingdom of God.

In our modern experience, every power tool must have a power source. Jesus consistently revealed the source of His healing power. In Matthew 17, Jesus encountered a boy who was demonized. The Bible says the boy was "lunatick" (Matt. 17:15). A demonic spirit was damaging his mind and afflicting the boy. The boy was brought to the disciples, who were unable to minister healing to him.

Then Jesus responded in a unique way, saying, "O faith-less and perverse generation, how long shall I be with you?" (Matt. 17:17). This question indicates Jesus' frustration. But why was He frustrated? It was because His disciples were not connecting to the source that was right in front of them. They did not tap into it because they did not use their faith.

Knowing the source is critical. But, faith is needed to tap into the source. In fact, faith in the power and anoint-ing of God is all we need to receive or minister healing in any situation. As Jesus' earthly ministry revealed, He not only has the power and the will to heal, but He also reveals the source of healing, which is the Holy Spirit. It is up to us to use the faith (in God and His power) that is supplied by His Spirit.

Call upon The Faith in The power and anointing of God

HIS DIVINE "RECIPE"

Jesus was the Anointed One "who went about doing good and healing all those who were oppressed of the devil..." (Acts 10:38).

God has revealed to us His divine recipe: the power, the will, and the source of healing. If we apply these truths to our lives, we will be confident that God is able to heal us, and we will be well supplied with the grace to walk in this reality.

In addition, there is the simple fact that Jesus died on the cross, defeated Satan, and rose again the third day to bring us to a place where we could walk in the covenant blessing of divine healing. The same Spirit that raised Jesus

Christ from the dead dwells on the inside of us (see Rom. 8:11). The anointing that was upon Jesus, healing the sick and raising the dead, is the same anointing that is on the inside of us (see 1 John 2:27).

We know that God is the Healer, because Christ is the Healer, and the Father and Son are one. We also know that we have all the tools we need to make divine healing and divine health realities in our lives right now!

POWER IN PRAYER

Thank You, Father, for revealing the aspects of healing demonstrated in Jesus' earthly ministry. I believe the record of Your Word. I know You have the power to heal every sickness and disease. I am so grateful to know that it is Your desire to heal all who are sick. And I know that the source of healing power is the Holy Spirit. Thank You for revealing Your nature and ways, so that I can resist the works of darkness, in my life and in the lives of others! In Jesus' name. Amen.

CHAPTER 5

Healing and the Passover

In Exodus 12, the Lord instructed Moses and Aaron, saying:

> *This month shall be unto you the beginning of months: it shall be the first month of the year to you. Speak ye unto all the congregation of Israel, saying, In the tenth day of this month they shall take to them every man a lamb, according to the house of their fathers, a lamb for an house...* (Exodus 12:2-3).

This was the beginning of the covenant institution known as Passover.

Toward the end of Israel's captivity in Egypt, God condemned the Egyptians with one last plague: the death of the firstborn. This plague represented God's judgment on the pagan world system. Yahweh warned Pharaoh to let His people go. After Pharaoh refused to conform to God's plan, God pronounced judgment on Egypt.

The death of the firstborn was very significant, because in a patriarchal society, the continuance of the kingdom was dependent upon the firstborn son.

God cut off the generations of Egypt, and in Exodus 12, He instituted a new system. He told the leadership of Israel that this was their first day of the year—a new day, a new system, and a new relationship. They were moving from judgment to exoneration, from bondage to freedom, from death to life. They were about to consummate their exodus from the Egyptian system.

Before they departed the land of their captivity, God told the Israelites exactly what He wanted them to do concerning the last plague. He commanded every household to prepare one lamb. This applied to all the children of Israel. God was so insistent upon every Israelite's participation, that He instructed smaller households to share a lamb between them.

In all cases, the lamb had to be without spot or blemish, and it had to be a male. The lamb was to be kept until the fourteenth day. Biblically, the number fourteen is significant; it represents salvation and deliverance. It also implies the full manifestation or double portion. After fourteen days the lamb was to be killed by the whole assembly of Israel, in the evening. They were then to take the blood and strike it against the upper doorpost and the lintels.

Let me take a moment and explain the symbolism. The last plague represented the destruction of the Egyptian system and the liberation of the children of Israel. God is a just God who cannot lie; therefore He could not discriminate in His judgment. The spirit of death released against the firstborn was assigned to kill all the firstborn in Egypt;

therefore, God had to provide a substitute sacrifice for the firstborn of Israel.

This was the provision God made for Israel: a firstborn male lamb that would take their place in the judgment. All firstborn Egyptians were to be destroyed, but God's divine plan preserved His people, Israel. Through the lamb, He provided for Israel's deliverance in its fullness—not a partial deliverance, but complete deliverance.

The Israelites were instructed to roast the remaining lamb with fire and eat it with unleavened bread. Leaven represents sin and the contamination of the world system. As they ate, their feet were sandaled and their loins were girded. They would leave Egypt swiftly—delivered in an instant. This is the Passover. This is the memorial given to Israel to remember their exodus.

COVENANT BLESSING OF HEALING

For years, I have studied and even taught on the Passover. It was not until recently that I realized that the Passover contained a spiritual mystery that uncovers the heart of God for divine healing. Psalms 105:37 explains: "He brought them forth also with silver and gold: and there was not one feeble person among their tribes."

The word *feeble* in this verse means "stumble" or "totter" (Strong, H3782). How interesting! The verse says that there was not one feeble person among millions. In the natural, this does not make sense. Typically, an enslaved group of people would include many who were sick due to their living conditions, oppression, diet, and many other factors. Imagine how many people would be sick after 430 years of bondage.

There must have been amputees, lepers, and diseased folks among them. How then can the Bible say that there were none sick? The mystery of this passage is contained within the observance of the Passover. There were probably hundreds sick in their midst—until they took the Passover.

By obeying God's instructions for the Passover, the children of Israel released His supernatural power to heal their bodies. They tapped into the mystery of the "substituting sacrifice." This concept would follow the Jewish people the rest of their days. The Israelites did not receive judgment because the lambs took the judgment in their place. The moment they ate of the sacrificial lamb, they received health, wholeness, and strength in their physical bodies.

The Passover was a covenant of blessing. By taking it according to the pattern that God set forth, the Israelites released covenant blessing into their bodies. This blessing strengthened them and empowered them, to the point that they left Egypt completely whole and restored.

This is why God told them in Exodus 15:26: "I am the LORD that healeth thee." He said He would put on Israel none of the diseases suffered by the Egyptians. Through the Passover, God restored them for their exodus and promised to be their Healer, as long as they kept His statutes.

Sickness was never supposed to affect God's people. Sickness and disease belong to this world system. The instant the Israelites stepped into God's system, they entered into health and wholeness. When God revealed

Himself as Jehovah Rapha, He promised to continue to be their Healer.

When you and I understand that God is interested in our wholeness and restoration, and that He instituted healing in the Passover, we can tap into this great mystery and be empowered.

HEALING IN THE COMMUNION

God has given us a rite to mark the sacrifice of His perfect Lamb:

> *For I have received of the Lord that which also I delivered unto you, that the Lord Jesus the same night in which he was betrayed took bread: and when he had given thanks, he brake it, and said, Take, eat: this is my body, which is broken for you: this do in remembrance of me. After the same manner also he took the cup, when he had supped, saying, This cup is the new testament in my blood: this do ye, as oft as ye drink it, in remembrance of me* (1 Corinthians 11:23-25).

Christ is our Passover lamb. He was typified in the Old Testament, in Exodus, and realized in the New Testament through His death, burial, and resurrection.

Like the Israelites of old, we were in bondage to an oppressive world system ruled by Satan. In First Corinthians, the apostle Paul describes the Last Supper, in which Christ affirmed that He is the Lamb, the substitutionary sacrifice for our sins. Jesus said that His body was broken for us. Just as the lamb was slain in Exodus 12, Jesus was slain for us—not under the Mosaic Covenant, but a new and better covenant containing eternal blessings.

Jesus also declared that His blood is the blood of the New Covenant shed for us. Christ was the blood of the lamb on the doorposts of the Israelites that turned away death from them. Jesus declared all these things while observing the traditional Passover of the Jewish people. In this, we see that He is the fulfillment of Passover.

This has tremendous implications for the New Covenant believer. It represents complete salvation and restoration. Not only were the Jews delivered out of Egypt, but they were also healed in their bodies. Communion provides the same blessing, but in greater measure. The Jews were healed as long as they kept God's statutes; but you and I were healed once and for all in Christ.

Many churches in America today do not a have a clue about the spiritual implications of Communion, just as many followers of Judaism do not understand the significance of Christ in the Passover (the fullness of Yahweh).

Paul says that whoever eats and drinks this cup of the Lord unworthily "shall be guilty of the body and blood of the Lord" (1 Cor. 11:27). He goes on to say that "for this cause many are weak and sickly among you, and many sleep" (1 Cor. 11:30).

For what reason do they sleep? For "not discerning the Lord's body" (1 Cor. 11:29). What does Paul mean by this? The word translated "discerning" here is the Greek word *diakrinō*, which means "to separate" or "make a distinction"

(Strong, G1252). This word is also used in Matthew 16:3 where Jesus rebukes the Pharisees, saying, "O ye hypocrites, ye can discern the face of the sky; but can ye not discern the signs of the times?" Here Jesus criticizes the Pharisees for being able to look at the sky and know what is coming in the weather, but not applying the same skills to understanding God's Kingdom.

To discern, then, means to rightly understand or respect something. We are to recognize the significance of the Communion. Paul says many are weak and sickly because they lack this understanding of the body and blood of Jesus. This is not just about being condemned because of sin. The text from First Corinthians 11 deals with people suffering unnecessarily because they do not grasp the magnitude of Christ's body and blood. They do not recognize that He was and is the perfect sacrifice for sin, and that, through Him, God has destroyed the works of Satan in the lives of believers, once and for all.

He is the Passover Lamb who has caused the spirit of sickness, poverty, and death to pass over us forever. We no longer have to be bound, but we can be free in Christ to worship Jehovah for eternity. Christ is our only defense against sickness and disease. He is the shelter we ran into for refuge.

There are many born-again, Spirit-filled believers who are being tormented because they do not recognize the true significance of the Communion. Every time we take the Communion of the body and blood of Jesus Christ, we are releasing divine healing. It does not matter what the sickness or disease may be, Christ overcame it. Every time we take Communion, we testify of His victory and demonstrate His supernatural power.

A COMMUNION TESTIMONY

While my wife was pregnant with our third child, she was diagnosed with gestational diabetes. This was very irritating for us, seeing that we are people of faith. When we received the news, we began to pray. I declared to my wife that she was healed, and she agreed. I went on further to tell her that she would go to the doctor's office and hear a reversal of this evil report.

Between the time we were given the news and the time she returned to the doctor, my wife and I and a few family members had devotionals in the morning. On a particular morning, we took Communion and declared that my wife was healed. We thanked God for the victory. On her next doctor's visit, her blood test came back negative for diabetes. Praise the living Jesus!

It is amazing how the simple act of partaking of the bread and wine (juice) could have such a tremendous spiritual impact on us. It is a further picture of the healing plan of God in Christ.

We have heard of and experienced countless testimonies of people receiving their healing through Communion. It is not just the act of taking Communion, but the revelation behind the Communion that releases the healing power of Christ. It all goes back to our understanding. The Bible says that we must eat with reverence. Reverence only comes from revelation. Unless we have revelation of who God is, we will never reverence Him. Until we have revelation of the body and blood of Jesus Christ, we will not have reverence for what is commonly known as Communion.

If you and I would only embrace and possess the fullness of the cross of Christ and His subsequent resurrection, we would be in such a powerful posture. Do you realize that every stripe on the back of Christ addressed a specific sickness or disease? Jesus said that His body was broken for us (see 1 Cor. 11:24). It was broken for us so that our bodies would be restored. He endured afflictions so that we no longer would be afflicted. Jesus said that His blood was shed for us (see Luke 22:20). This represented both atonement and covenant. He paid the penalty for our sins and brought us into a New Covenant relationship. This covenant relationship has blessings attached to it.

When believers catch hold of this truth, sickness and disease do not stand a chance against them. The greatest embodiment of God's redemptive plan is the body and blood of Jesus Christ as represented in Communion. Every time we take it in faith and understanding, we give the devil a black eye. We remind him that there is nothing we have ever done in our lives that the blood of Jesus is not able to cover. Neither is there any sickness that was not addressed in His body.

The more we partake of this memorial the more we enter into the consciousness of the finished work—and it is the consciousness of the finished work that produces results in our lives. It does not matter how disillusioned you may be with sickness, you must remind yourself that His body was broken *for you*. His blood was shed *for you*.

POWER IN PRAYER

Thank You, Jesus, for all You have done—for me! Your precious body was broken for me, and Your blood was shed for me. Therefore I take authority over any and all forms of sickness and disease and I declare that they are not permitted to live here anymore! In Jesus' name. Amen.

CHAPTER 6

Healing Versus Feeling

*Who his own self bare our sins in his own
body on the tree, that we, being dead to sins,
should live unto righteousness: by whose
stripes ye were healed* (1 Peter 2:24).

Oftentimes people struggle with the notion of being healed because they do not feel like they are healed. Quite frankly, healing is not a feeling.

The word for "healed" in First Peter 2:24 is *iaomai*, which means: "to cure" or "make whole" (Strong, G2390). This healing is an act of God's grace manifested in Christ. It occurred in the past tense. First Peter 2:24 does not say that He *will* heal us; it says we *were* healed. This is very important to understand.

When Christ hung on the cross dying for the sins of humanity more than two thousand years ago, He was reconciling the world to Himself. He was *healing* us. The Bible says:

To wit, that God was in Christ, reconciling the world unto himself, not imputing their trespasses unto them; and hath committed unto us the word of reconciliation (2 Corinthians 5:19).

Christ reconciled the world. What does that mean? The word translated "reconciling" is the Greek word *katallassō*, which literally means to "exchange" or "return to favour with" (Strong, G2644). This word is used largely in a monetary sense. It means to exchange coins or to engage in a transaction that restores someone to favor. In other words, Christ paid the penalty that we owed God, and in return we were restored to a favorable position with Him.

Peter writes that in the process of this transaction, you and I were healed, or cured. Simply put, healing has nothing to do with us, and everything to do with Him! Many Christians believe that they are the ones who bring about their healing through their own goodness or religious works. That has nothing to do with it at all. In fact, the only reason it is possible for you and me to walk in divine healing is because of the reconciling work of the cross of Christ.

Our healing is a done deal. The price was already paid. The money has already changed hands. Whether or not you and I feel healed is completely irrelevant. Our healing is as much a reality as the sun rising every morning. Whether it feels hot or not has no bearing on the reality of the sun's existence. Even in the winter when the temperature is at its coldest, the sun still rises every morning.

The Bible does not say that "by His stripes ye *feel* healed." It says "by [His] stripes ye *were* healed" (1 Pet. 2:24). This is known as a biblical truth, or a biblical reality. The absolute truth is that we were healed of any and every disease on the cross of Calvary.

Second Corinthians 5:19 uses the phrase "and hath committed unto us the word of reconciliation." The English phrase "word of reconciliation" combines two words in the Greek: *logos* and *katallage,* implying a decree or mandate of exchange or favor (Strong, G3056).

This is a sovereign declaration. It means that God has given us His Word that reconciliation has taken place. In other words, we can bet our bottom dollar on it.

Not only that, but He wants us to proclaim this Word to everyone around us. We have been reconciled to God in the person of Jesus Christ. For this reason you and I have a right to walk in the benefits of that reconciliation. It is a fixed reality. It is the truth.

TESTIMONY: LYING SYMPTOMS (MS)

Let me share a brief testimony with you: About a year and a half ago, a close relative of mine was diagnosed with advanced multiple sclerosis, a nervous system disorder. When this happened I was very much taken aback. I knew that it was an attack from Satan, but what I did not know is that Satan was trying to attack me as well.

Shortly after I heard this news, I began to experience symptoms similar to what a person with a neurological or nervous system disorder would experience. My legs began to go numb for days at a time. My face began to spasm uncontrollably. I could not feel the tips of my fingers.

I was a bit concerned, to say the least. Then the enemy began to sow seeds of fear into my mind and tell me that I was also going to be diagnosed with an illness. After a few days I decided to take the offensive. I read every scripture in the Bible on healing. I meditated on the scriptures every single day.

Once I began to realize the truth of the Word of God, I started to stand on the authority of that Word. Instead of asking God to heal me, I began to thank Him that I was already healed—two thousand years ago when my healing was manifested on the cross. As I began to praise God and thank Him for perfect health, every symptom began to disappear. I have not experienced any of those symptoms since.

The point of the story is that I did not feel healed. But healing is not a feeling; it is the truth. It is God's reality, which is the only reality that matters. It is great to go to crusades and feel a touch from the Lord, but the truth of the matter is that you don't need to feel a touch to walk in divine healing. All you have to do is believe the simple truth: you are healed! You are not *going to be* healed, you *are* healed.

UNLIMITED BY THE PHYSICAL WORLD

It does not matter what the sickness or symptom is; God has already addressed it in Christ on the cross. The challenge that we face is that we live in a physical world. So much of what we experience has its basis in what we can see, touch, taste, and feel. It is important to understand that feelings can be very deceiving.

For example, have you ever been overwhelmed by fear? It has a paralyzing effect on your whole body. Your senses are all distorted based on that one emotion. Satan's greatest attacks are in the sense realm. He loves to exploit what we can see, touch, taste, and feel. As a matter of fact, the Bible refers to him as "the god of this world" (2 Cor. 4:4).

In the fourth chapter of the Gospel of Luke, Jesus returned from His baptism in the Jordan River, and was led into the wilderness to fast for forty days and forty nights. After forty days of this, He was fatigued.

You must understand scientifically that when you are fasting, the body depletes itself of carbohydrates. This causes the loss of appetite after just three days. After forty days without eating, the body enters starvation mode.

Simply put; Jesus was starving to death, and Satan came to tempt Him. The Bible says in Luke 4:3: "And the devil said unto him, If thou be the Son of God, command this stone that it be made bread."

Satan tried to get Jesus to be confined by the realm of His physical senses. Jesus replied: "It is written, That man shall not live by bread alone, but by *every word of God*" (Luke 4:4). Jesus responded to Satan by telling him that man should not be solely dependent on the physical realm for his sustenance. Instead, he should depend on every word of God.

Matthew 4:4 quotes Jesus' words this way: "Man shall not live by bread alone, but by every word that proceedeth out of the mouth of God." In the Greek, Jesus literally said that man should not live by physical food but by every *rhema* of God. In other words, Jesus was referring, not to the written Word, but the spoken Word.

Rhema is a Greek word that signifies "that which is or has been uttered by the living voice...spoken word" (Strong, G4487). This is a very important concept that Jesus introduced in scripture. He is saying that you and I are not to be confined by the physical realm; we are to live by the *rhema* Word of God. We live based on the Word of God that the Holy Spirit speaks to us. That Word is our reality. Even though Jesus was starving in the physical realm, He was full of the Word in the spiritual realm and that Word sustained His physical weakness.

As we meditate on God's Word concerning the promise of healing, that Word becomes a living voice on the inside of us. It will supersede and override every other voice that speaks to us. The reason Jesus could resist the devil in His physical temptation was because the voice of God on the inside of Him was louder than the voice He heard on the outside. He was not operating by what He felt, but on the basis of the living voice of the Word of God.

The voice we listen to becomes our reality.

WE MUST MAKE A DECISION

Every time we are faced with challenges in our bodies we have to decide what the truth is: Is it what we feel or what God says? I have decided to stand on the truth of God's Word, not what I feel. This is the key to everything in the Kingdom of God: our ability to discern, believe, and act upon the truth. In John 8:32 Jesus says: "And you shall *know* the truth, and the truth shall make you free."

This is one of the most profound and most overlooked scriptures in the Bible.

The word translated "know" is the Greek word *ginōskō* which means to have a deep understanding or to be intimately acquainted with (Strong, G1097). It was a Jewish idiom which literally implied intercourse. In the Old Testament, we read that "Adam *knew* Eve his wife; and she conceived..." (Gen. 4:1). The idea in John 8:32 is that the truth is to impregnate us.

God wants His Word to be planted on the inside of us and produce fruit. We are to be pregnant with the truth. The truth alone will not liberate a person. But to the extent that we know the truth, it will have the power to produce freedom in our lives. Many people can quote the Bible, but that does not mean that they *know the truth*. It is not a reality for them; it is simply religious jargon. The true test of whether or not we know God's Word is how we respond in the midst of challenges. When situations place pressure on that Word which we claim to believe, our responses serve as barometers measuring the level to which we are impregnated by that Word.

Jesus was full of the Word of God. It was alive and active on the inside of Him. The evidence of this was His ability to stand strong in the midst of His temptation in the wilderness.

WHAT IS TRUTH?

One might ask the question: What is truth? In John 8:32 the Greek word *alētheia* is translated "truth." It means: "what is true in any matter under consideration" (Strong, G225). It is that which is objective in nature, unmovable, unshakable, and without pretense.

In short, Jesus is the truth. He is the personification of truth. He is the Word of God incarnate; therefore, the Word of God is the truth. This truth has nothing to do with facts, but it has everything to do with what God says. Whatever the Word of God says is the truth.

In order for the truth to liberate us, we must know what the truth says. When God makes a promise in His Word, that promise is unshakable and unmovable. It does not matter how things look on the outside, or what people say, or how you feel; the Word of God is your reality.

The Word supersedes every external factor. The sooner we understand this concept, the sooner we will live above the realm of our feelings. Healing is not a matter of how we feel on the outside; it is a matter of believing what God says on the inside.

INTERNALIZE THE WORD

The Word of God that is internalized and that speaks actively to us is the power that will bring liberation from the oppression of sickness.

When you are faced with a symptom in your body, you must appropriate the Word of God down on the inside of you, and act on that Word alone. Say to yourself what Jesus said to Satan, "I do not live by bread alone, but by every word (*rhema*) that proceeds from the mouth of God. I am not moved by what I feel, but I know the truth of God's Word, and that truth has made me free." AWESOME

You must never underestimate the power of confessing the Word of God, especially in the midst of feelings that are contrary to the Word. So many people allow their feelings to rule over them: this is not the will of God for your life! God wants a people who are determined that whatever He says is true no matter what they see, hear, or feel on the outside. Jesus was our example of the power of the truth. He knew the truth; He was pregnant with the Word, and that Word governed His actions! Do it

Instead of complaining and crying about what is going on in your body, begin to study, meditate on, and confess the Word of God. Enroll yourself in a "Word Clinic." Whatever is causing pain in your body, mind, or soul, apply God's Word to it like medicine. It does not matter what the condition is. Apply the healing ointment of God's Word to it, and watch your healing manifest.

Make up your mind that you will not be governed by your feelings, but you will be controlled by the Word of God and the Word of God alone. Allow the Word of God to dictate your feelings, not the other way around. Remember, there is only one truth, and it has nothing to do with how you feel: it has everything to do with what God says.

POWER IN PRAYER

Father I declare that there is only one truth: Your Word. I acknowledge Your holy Word as the highest and final authority in my life. I declare that all of my feelings and emotions must bow to Your Word. I am not motivated by what I see, hear or feel; I am only motivated by the Word of God. I recognize that Your Word is Your will for my life. I can rely on Your Word for anything that pertains to me. I am the healed of the Lord because Your Word declares that I am. Thank You, Lord, for transforming my thinking from being governed by my feelings to being governed by Your Word. In Jesus' name. Amen.

CHAPTER 7

Rise, Take up Your Bed, and Walk

Jesus saith unto him, Rise, take up thy bed, and walk (John 5:8)

The Gospels give us remarkable examples of the healing power of Jesus. There are numerous accounts of Jesus healing the sick. If you ever needed encouragement on whether or not Jesus was the Healer, simply read the Gospels of Matthew, Mark, Luke, and John.

Surprisingly, John's Gospel gives the fewest accounts of healing miracles, but there is one example in John's Gospel that gives the perfect theological and practical display of healing in the Bible.

THE POOL OF BETHESDA

In John chapter 5, Jesus went to Jerusalem for the Feast of the Jews, and arrived at the pool called Bethesda. The word *Bethesda* in Hebrew means "house of mercy" (Strong, G964). This is significant because it reveals to us God's agenda concerning healing, and displays God's loving-kindness and compassion. It shows us a picture of the Father's heart.

As we have already seen, the operation of faith is based on the knowledge of God's will: the more you know about the will of God concerning your life, the stronger your faith becomes. At the pool of Bethesda, Jesus found many sick, blind, impotent, halt, and withered people waiting for the moving of the waters. They believed, and the Bible records, that at a certain season, an angel went to the pool and stirred the water. Anyone who stepped in was healed of whatever disease or condition they had.

The amazing thing is that the people intrinsically knew that sickness was not an acceptable thing. In our culture today we have accepted sickness as a way of life. We have literally come into agreement with it. At least back then the people had enough sense to know that they could not stay in their situation: there was something better!

At the pool, Jesus found a man who had been crippled for thirty-eight years. Knowing the man had been there for a very long time, Jesus asked him a profound question: "Will thou be made whole?" (John 5:6).

This is a powerful question for several reasons. Number one: it examined the motive of the man's heart. Many people say they want healing, but in truth they have become content in their situations. This man was at that very place in his own life. He replied to Jesus' question by saying, "I don't have anyone to help me, and every time I try to get in the pool, someone goes in front of me" (see John 5:7).

This is where many people are in their lives. They are making excuses for the condition they are in. They blame everyone else. They blame time: "I have been here so long!" They blame people: "So-and-so hurt me. This is why I am sick." They blame circumstances: "I couldn't get to the healing line!" Unfortunately, those are illegitimate excuses. They are the reason Jesus questioned the man's motive.

The second purpose of Jesus' question was to challenge the man's will. No matter how we look at it, faith always involves volition. We have to exercise our will in order for faith to work. So before Jesus addressed anything related to the impotent man's physical condition, He addressed his will.

Having already tested the man's motive, Jesus now challenged his mindset. Our mindsets are very important when it comes to healing. The impotent man had a victim mentality. He was waiting on God and people to do something for him. Beloved, many people have gone to the grave waiting for their circumstances to change. In fact, God has already made all provision for healing to be manifested in our lives. *He is waiting on us.*

The third dimension to Jesus' question—"Will thou be made whole?"—was a call to wholeness. Sometimes it is not enough to just get into a better situation than the one we are in right now. God wants us to be more than changed; He wants us whole. This is a vital key in the Christian experience.

Just as much as God wants us to experience the blessings and benefits He has for us; He wants us to desire them to be manifested in our lives. Any good father wants his children to desire his involvement in their lives. To some degree, it is a dimension of the Father heart of God to want us to desire His best for our lives.

It is possible that until Jesus posed His pointed question, the impotent man may have forgotten the prospect of wholeness. Life has a way of causing us to lose hope in the promises of God. But we can choose to hang onto them!

TIME IS NOT A FACTOR

Some people believe that because they have been in their circumstance for a length of time, there is no way the situation could ever change.

Nothing could be further from the truth! The length of time you have been in your situation has no bearing on the power of God. The only factor that matters is your willingness to believe God's Word.

This impotent man was posed a serious question: "Wilt thou be made whole?" God is asking us the same question today. We must make up our minds what we want before we can truly embrace anything that God has to offer. James 1:8: says: "A double minded man is unstable in all his ways." Double-mindedness prevents our receiving from God. We have to make up our minds that we want what God says belongs to us.

Two of the biggest contributors to double-mindedness are ignorance of the Word of God and false teaching.

When we are ignorant of God's promises, we are unable to confidently expect those promises to be manifested in our lives. If we are sitting under false teaching that says it is the perfect will of God for us to be sick, then we are incapable of receiving healing from God.

When these factors are working, we have two minds. The Greek word translated "double minded" in James 1:8 is *dipsychos*, which means to have a divided interest or to be uncertain (Strong, G1374).

Many people in the Church are this way; their interests are divided. One day they are asking God to heal them; the next day they are telling Him, *"If* it be Thy will." They are quite literally confused.

When we are in this predicament it is difficult for us to stand firm and appropriate the promises of God for our lives.

RISE!

The next statement Jesus made to the impotent man at the pool may have surprised some. He said, "Rise, take up thy bed, and *walk!*" (John 5:8).

Let us take a moment and examine Jesus' words. The first command to the impotent man was: "Rise." This is the Greek word *egeirō*, which means "arouse from the sleep of death" (Strong, G1453); in other words, awaken from the dead.

The impotent man was in a place of emotional, spiritual, and physical death. Even though his faculties were working, he was as good as dead. This is a profound spiritual principle. When Jesus commanded the man to "Rise," it was an act of compassion. This word contained the life-giving power needed for the man to arise from his condition, awake from death, and stand.

Jesus' command was not based on the impotent man's ability; it was based on the ability of God's Word to give the man life.

IT'S NOT ABOUT YOUR ABILITY

Too many people attempt to obtain healing through their own ability. They are unaware of the potency of the Word of God. When we study and meditate on the Word of God we are sowing life-giving seed into our spirit man. That seed will produce results. If you notice, Jesus did not lay a single finger on the impotent man, He simply proclaimed the Word. He told the man, "Rise." This word was all he needed to break the bondage of his current situation.

The very words Jesus spoke became the life-giving force that enabled the man to exit his bedridden condition of thirty-eight years. The Word of God literally infused his entire body and went into the muscles and nervous system, giving life to dead cells.

He longs to do no less for us.

POWER IN PRAYER

Father, in accordance with Your Word, I decree and declare that I am made whole by the power of the Holy Spirit. Every arthritic condition that plagues my body is reversed because of Your Word, Lord Jesus. I also speak to my kidneys, liver, central nervous system, heart, brain, muscle tissue, immune system, lungs, white blood cells, bones, joints, and bone marrow, and declare that they rise up in health and strength this very moment. In Jesus' name. Amen.

CHAPTER 8

Faith Is the Key

And Jesus answering saith unto them, Have faith in God. For verily I say unto you, That whosoever shall say unto this mountain, Be thou removed, and be thou cast into the sea; and shall not doubt in his heart, but shall believe that those things which he saith shall come to pass; he shall have whatsoever he saith (Mark 11:22-23).

One of the most important aspects of our ability to receive and walk in divine healing is faith. Faith is paramount to the Christian life. It is through faith that we are positioned to experience the benefits and blessings of God. Interestingly enough, faith is very simple, but very misunderstood. I would dare to say that faith is one of the most misunderstood subjects in the Church.

There has been much teaching about faith in recent years, and it seems that some of it has done more harm than good. In the book of Mark, Jesus told His disciples,

"Have faith in God." Literally, in the Greek He was telling them to "Have the faith *of* God." The word used for "faith" here is the word *pistis*, which includes the idea of confidence, and "conviction of the truth of anything," specifically God in this case (Strong, G4102).

Simply put, faith is confidence in God's Word. When we are walking in faith, we are convinced that God is exactly who He says He is, and will do exactly what He says He will do.

THE RHEMA WORD

The question is: how do we obtain faith? In Luke 4, when Jesus was tempted by Satan in the Perean wilderness, Satan attempted to provoke Him, saying, "If thou be the Son of God, command this stone that it be made bread" (Luke 4:3). In the next verse, Jesus responded by saying, "It is written, That man shall not live by bread alone, but by every word of God." In this one statement by Jesus, we find a key that unlocks the power of faith.

Satan was testing the authenticity of the person of Jesus Christ. There was no question as to whether or not Jesus was the Son of God. But Jesus was not about to betray His humanity to prove anything to Satan. Jesus had to fulfill His earthly ministry as the Son of Man. He responded to Satan by saying that man should not live by bread alone but by every word that proceeds out of the mouth of God (see Matt. 4:4). In this case, Jesus used the Greek word *rhema* to describe the Word of God.

We have already seen that the word *rhema* refers to "the living voice." Jesus was declaring to the devil and to us that God's Word is more than black-and-white print; it is meant to be alive and active on the inside of us.

HEARING THE WORDS WE READ

It is not enough to read the Bible; we must *hear* the revelation of the Holy Spirit from the words that we read. Simply put, we have to have revelation. Romans 10:17 says that faith comes by hearing and hearing comes by the word—the *rhema*—of God. It is significant that the Bible uses the same word in Luke 4:4 and Romans 10:17.

The way we obtain faith is from the Word of God. The more we eat, or take in, the bread of the Word, the more the Holy Spirit speaks to us concerning that Word, and the more revelation we receive. The reason Jesus was able to resist the devil after fasting for forty days in the desert was not just because He was God, but because He had a revelation of God as His source of strength and power. He was convinced about God's Word. The Word was alive and active on the inside of Jesus.

The more we meditate on the Word of God, the more we have confidence in the Word. Faith can only operate where the will of God is known and acted upon. When we are ignorant of God's will, we cannot exercise real faith.

Several years ago I had a conversation with a friend who asked me, "Why would God heal some people and not others? Is it possible that it is not His will to heal those who don't get healed?

This was a very heated discussion because he brought out the fact that some people have believed God for their healing and still died. This issue has become a "sacred cow" in the Church today. Many denominations even discourage the teaching of faith for this very reason. The real question implied is whether or not the Word of God is absolutely true.

The most dangerous thing Christians can do is to measure God based on other Christians' experiences. God can only be measured by His Word. Just because people have died after saying they believed God for their healing does not mean that God is not who He says He is.

The problem is unbelief. Just because people say they believe the Word of God does not mean that they really do. Faith is not about quoting scripture, or having an emotional response. Faith is *conviction* based on the authority of God's Word. *Conviction* is defined as an "unshakable belief in something without need for proof or evidence."

Simply put, real faith is not moved by what we see or feel; it is solely based on God's Word. It is more than just naming it and claiming it. It is not just about positively affirming the things that we desire. It is the Word of God. Walking in faith is about having a revelation by the Spirit of God that the Word of God is absolutely true, to the point that we will take action because of it.

Hebrews 11:1 says: "Now faith is the substance of things hoped for, the evidence of things not seen." The word for "substance" is the Greek word *hupostasis*, which conveys the idea of support, or more literally, "substructure" (Strong, G5287).

In other words, our faith is what we stand upon. Many people have learned, through certain faith movements in the Church, to talk by faith; but they still don't understand how to walk by faith. Bible faith is not mental assent. Real Bible faith is a revelation based on the Word of God. We can stand upon it. Faith is the substantiation of what we believe.

This is one of the most important truths of scripture, because everything about our ability to know and receive from God is based on faith. We believe that we are healed because God says that we are. We believe that we can stand on God's Word because God says that it is a sure foundation.

Here is another way of describing faith: it is the title deed to what we have been promised. It is the evidentiary proof of ownership that guarantees that you and I will receive the manifestation of God's Word in our lives.

HEALING IS NOT A FUTURE EVENT

All that being said, why do people find it so difficult to believe God for their healing?

Simple! They see it as a future event. They don't realize that it has already taken place. Jesus already paid the price for our healing. When you and I stand on the Word of God, we are placing a demand on the finished work of Christ to be manifested in our lives.

God is not *going to* heal anyone! Asking God to heal you is like purchasing a brand-new vehicle from the factory and wishing and hoping that you can use it one day. The only thing that will make driving that car a reality is putting the key in the ignition and activating it. The car has everything it needs to accomplish all that it was manufactured to do. But you have to have the key to activate all of its features.

Faith is the key!

POWER IN PRAYER

Father, thank You for Your Word. Because it is trustworthy and true, I have confidence in it. Therefore, I stand upon the substance and substructure of Your Word, convinced that all You have promised has already been accomplished through the finished work of the cross of Christ. I take Your Word to heart—thank You for showing me how I should act on it. I place a demand, today, upon that finished work, fully expecting to see it manifested in every area of my life. In Jesus' name. Amen.

CHAPTER 9

Confess the Word

That if thou shalt confess with thy mouth the Lord Jesus, and shalt believe in thine heart that God hath raised him from the dead, thou shalt be saved (Romans 10:9).

The Word of God makes it clear that confession is an integral part of the Christian experience. As a matter of fact, it is one of the primary dimensions of the born-again experience.

In Romans 10:9, the word rendered "confess" is the Greek word *homologeo*. In essence, it means to say what has already been said (Strong, G3670). The idea is to admit and agree with someone or something verbally.

You may ask what this has to do with healing. My answer is: *everything*. The Bible says that true confession is an outflow of our belief system. Paul the apostle asserts in Second Corinthians 4:13 that we believe and therefore we speak.

It is not enough for us to say we believe that Christ died on the cross for our sins and our healing. We must also say what the Word of God says. One of the biggest problems in the Church is that people who profess to be born-again believers often find themselves saying the opposite of what God says.

Before there can be sincere confession there must be agreement with the Word of God. When we agree with the Word of God, we are saying that He is right and everything and everyone else is wrong. No matter what religion and tradition say, the Word of God must be the final authority in the life of a believer. Therein lies much of the difficulty; many people have not made up their minds and are not convinced in their hearts that God's Word is absolute truth.

CONFESS AND BELIEVE

Confessing the Word of God is a declaration that we fully agree with it and are submitted to its authority. This is where the battle rages: in the heart and in the mouth. The Bible says that we are to confess with our mouths and believe in our hearts (see Rom. 10:9). These two must work in concert with one another to produce the desired outcome: salvation.

Salvation has many implications, but for the purpose of this chapter we will utilize the most basic application of the word, which is the Greek word *sozo*. It is translated "saved" in Romans 10:9. *Sozo* means "to save, i.e. deliver or protect..." (Strong, G4982).

The idea of salvation goes beyond a simple moral transformation. It implies a deliverance and/or restoration from evil and peril. In this sense salvation also applies to sickness. Through Christ's death, God not only delivered humanity from the curse of sin passed down through Adam; but He also delivered us from its effects: death, poverty, and sickness.

To confess and believe is to come into agreement and alignment with this biblical truth. When a person confesses that Jesus Christ is Lord and has risen from the dead, they are asserting that the Word of God is true. They are relinquishing control of their lives to Jesus, and they are declaring His Lordship over circumstances.

This means that when sickness touches your life, it is violating your covenant relationship with God. Sickness is an intruder.

THE AUTHORITY OF THE WORD

The place from which we believe and submit to the Word of God, and declare that Word out of our mouths, is the place of power and authority. This is why Satan fights against our consistent confession of the Word: he recognizes its power. In recent years there has been an attempt to discredit confession through scandal and negative press concerning religious figures who utilize the principle. But that has nothing to do with the truth of the Word of God.

We must be very watchful not to jump on Satan's bandwagon. If the Word of God says it, you ought to believe it, and that should settle it!

I heard a popular minister say on television: "We have to be balanced, now! Don't go off on the deep end now!" I beg to differ. There is nowhere in the Word of God that tells Christians to be balanced. Faith is radical! It looks like absolute foolishness to the world.

I believe this is why many Christians never receive their healing—because they reject the truth of scripture in the name of being "balanced." This is simply a code word for fear. If Jesus had been balanced He would never have healed the blind or raised the dead or cast out devils. All of those things come from being completely sold out on the authority of the Word of God.

In order to appropriate healing in our lives, we must open our mouths and begin to declare over our lives exactly what the Word says. When the enemy comes to bring lying symptoms, we must declare the truth of God's Word to our bodies. We must speak it forth. We are not speaking arbitrarily; we are speaking what the Word says.

TESTIMONY: SINUSES HEALED

One of the members of our church was being attacked with sickness in his body in the form of sinus infections. His wife had been sitting under the Word for quite some time, and built her faith to a level where she was convinced that sickness was not the will of God. As her husband coughed and suffered in the middle of the night, she sat up in the bed with boldness and laid her hands on him.

She said, "Be healed, in Jesus' name!" and the coughing ceased. He began to cough once again and she again declared, "Be healed!" Needless to say, the coughing ceased and did not return.

We have seen and heard of countless instances like this. Satan does not want the Church to believe that healing is this simple. He does not want the Church to believe that our deliverance is in our mouths.

What if I told you that *your* healing is simply a confession away? What if I told you that no matter what you are facing in your body, the Word of God in your mouth is more than enough to bring about your deliverance?

It's true!

God created the universe with His spoken Word, and has ordained that we dominate the world He created with *our* words. Contained inside of the Word of God is the life-giving power needed to bring it to pass.

Speak over yourself. Declare with your mouth that you are the healed of the Lord—no matter what symptoms are present in your life.

It has been scientifically proven that speaking to plants helps them to grow. Why would speaking have any effect on plants? Plants are living organisms and God created all living things through His spoken Word. Therefore all living things are designed to respond to the spoken Word.

Our bodies are under that same dominion. When we want something to happen or to cease, we must speak to it. This is very useful, specifically in the area of cancerous growths and tumors. Say to that cancer or growth: "Cancer, I command you to cease and desist in the name of Jesus Christ. I curse you at your very roots."

TESTIMONY: CANCER DRIED UP BY THE ROOTS

A lady came to my wife and me for prayer. She had a growth on her back for a year and a half, and it had become cancerous. When she came forward for prayer, the anointing of the Holy Ghost fell on me and I told her that she "shall not die, but live, and declare the works of the LORD" (Ps. 118:17).

When I spoke this word over her she fell out in the Spirit. Two days later, during our Sunday morning service, we received a message from her that the cancerous growth withered and fell off her back in the shower.

Praise the Lord Jesus Christ! His Word will never return void (see Isa. 55:11). We must boldly confess the Word of God, no matter what the situation is.

POWER IN PRAYER

Father in the name of Jesus Christ, I come to You now as my Healer and my Deliverer. I confess Your Word in accordance with Romans 10:9-10. I believe that Your Word is absolutely true and that Your Word has restoration power. According to Your Word, I now confess that I am the healed of the Lord. My mouth only speaks forth that which glorifies You. I speak life out of my mouth, and that life permeates every fiber of my being. In Jesus' name. Amen.

CHAPTER 10

Sin's Effect on Healing

And the prayer of faith shall save the sick, and the Lord shall raise him up; and if he have committed sins, they shall be forgiven him (James 5:15).

A common misconception that we hear concerning healing is that sin will prevent the believer from being healed. This is neither scripturally nor logically sound.

Many people have been told by well-intentioned and not so well-intentioned leaders in the Church that the reason they are sick is because they have sin in their lives. It just does not match what the Word of God has to say. I will continue to reiterate that every theological belief that we hold must be based on the uncompromised Word of God. Many people say they believe the Word of God, but they try to nullify it through reason and logic.

You will never receive the blessing of healing by dismissing what the Word of God says concerning healing.

WHO SINNED?

In the Gospel of John, Jesus was asked by His disciples whether a particular man was born blind because of his parents' sin or his own sin (see John 9:2). At that time, people related all sickness to sin or evil.

Now it is important to note that all sickness originated from sin and is inherently evil because it is outside of the original plan of God. However, in the matter of this man, Jesus said something very interesting: "Neither hath this man sinned, nor his parents: but that the works of God should be made manifest in him" (John 9:3).

Here Jesus changed things up and presented a viewpoint that is both counter-religious and countercultural. They lived in a society of extreme self-righteousness and superstition. Yet Jesus deflated both of those paradigms.

The reason given for the blindness was not sin, but an opportunity for the works of God to be manifest. The man's condition was clearly an evil that needed to be addressed, but the man was not encouraged to have a mentality that made him feel unworthy of healing.

Well, did the sickness come from God? The Bible makes it emphatically clear through this passage. If God was the one responsible for the man's blindness then it would not say that the work of God should be made manifest, because the blindness itself would have been a work of God.

The same apostle John wrote the following in First John 3:8:

He that committeth sin is of the devil; for the devil sinneth from the beginning. For this purpose the Son of God was manifested, that he might destroy the works of the devil.

JESUS CAME TO DESTROY SICKNESS

Scripture says that Jesus came to destroy the works of the evil one. Blindness was a work of the evil one that needed to be destroyed. How was it destroyed? By Jesus manifesting the works of God in healing the blind man.

The important point here is that sin was by no means a barrier to Jesus' ability to heal. Many people have been convinced that they are sick because of sin; therefore, they will not even address the fact that they are dealing with the work of Satan in their lives.

Jesus was trying to get His disciples to see that it is not an issue of sin, but an issue of the power of God. You do not deserve to be sick. Do not accept sickness in your life! Acceptance of sickness on the basis of sin in your life will prevent you from being able to confidently appropriate the promises of God's Word.

In the book of James, this truth is driven home in a profound way. The fifth chapter of James makes a strong statement. First of all, it asks if there are any in the Church who are sick (see James 5:14). In that statement we have a picture of the early Church: the whole Church was not sick.

The second thing James says is to call the elders of the church (see James 5:14). This means that the people were not to be content in their sickness. Everyone in the early

Church knew that sickness was a bad thing. They were not told to accept it as the will of God. It is an atrocity for any leader in the Church to tell someone to accept his or her sickness as the will of God!

Next, James tells the believer to be anointed with oil, which represents the anointing of the Holy Spirit. Then, it says that the prayer of faith shall save the sick, and if he has committed any sins, they shall be forgiven. (See James 5:14-15).

This passage just burst someone's theological bubble. James does not tell us to get the sin out of our lives first; rather he says that the prayer of faith shall save the sick.

Now the word for "faith" there is the same word for faith used in Romans 10:17: it is the Greek word *pistis,* which involves confidence or conviction. In other words, it is the prayer of confidence that will bring salvation to the sick.

What must our confidence be in? The Word of God! Notice that it does not say that prayer will heal the sick, but it says it will *save* the sick. The word save is the same Greek word *sozo* that is used in Romans 10:9-10. It speaks of deliverance. The word *deliverance* implies rescue from evil or danger. As a matter of fact the word "sick" or "sickness" is often translated "evil" or "affliction" in the New Testament. In James 5:14, it speaks of "weakness" (Strong, G770).

SICKNESS IS EVIL

The word *deliverance* is used to illuminate the nature of sickness: it is inherently evil. Finally, the passage in James 5 tells us that if there are any sins in the sick person's life they shall be forgiven and the Lord shall raise him up (see James 5:15).

When we come to Christ, He does not ask us to remove the sin out of lives before we can be saved. Instead, we are saved from the bondage of sin when we come to Him in faith. He does the delivering. He destroys sin in our lives. We simply believe in the finished work and obey Him in response.

Healing is no different. The same process that saves a person also heals a person, and both involve the prayer of faith. Just like God forgives us of our sin in saving us, He also forgives us of our sin in healing us. It is in fact the same salvation at work in both instances.

To suggest that God will not heal you because there is sin in your life is ridiculous. What if a sinner came to the altar to give her life to Christ and we told her, "You have too much sin in your life to be saved"? That sounds ridiculous doesn't it?

We must remember that both salvation and healing are manifestations of the grace of God through the atoning sacrifice of Jesus Christ. If we come to God in faith, trusting in His Word, He will not only manifest healing in our lives, but He will also forgive us (and has already forgiven us) of our sins.

POWER IN PRAYER

Father in the name of Jesus Christ, I thank You for Your grace. Because I place my confidence in Your

Word, I receive healing, just as I received salvation. Jesus came to deliver me from the evils of sickness, just as surely as He came to forgive my sin. Thank You for manifesting Your grace in every area of my life. In Jesus' name. Amen.

CHAPTER 11

Healing and Forgiveness

*Therefore I say unto you, What things soever
ye desire, when ye pray, believe that ye receive
them, and ye shall have them. And when ye stand
praying, forgive, if ye have ought against any:
that your Father also which is in heaven may
forgive you your trespasses* (Mark 11:24-25).

What does healing have to do with forgiveness? This is one of those things that many people have taught on and discussed for many years. I have heard it said that many sicknesses can be attributed to an unwillingness to forgive. Though I believe this can be true, I don't believe this is the main issue when it comes to healing.

The Bible tells us in Mark 11:24 that whatever we desire when we pray (believing), we shall receive. This is an absolute statement.

Again, we have to be careful not to allow religion and tradition to dilute the Word of God. It means exactly what it says. Whatever we ask God for, He will give it to us. The only condition that must be met is to believe in your heart. Some people may say, "Well, what if it is outside of the will of God?" We cannot exercise real faith outside of the confines of God's will. Remember that faith is confidence in the Word of God.

The issue of forgiveness was significant enough for Jesus to address it in His own words. I have heard many try to say that His words about forgiveness do not apply to the New Testament believer because He had not yet gone to the cross when He spoke them. That is irresponsible and dismissive theology.

Jesus' words and teaching are quoted as biblical truth by many of the apostles throughout the epistles. We as New Testament believers are to live by these teachings. The vast majority of Jesus' words were stated before He went to the cross. The point is that we are not to dismiss the Word of God when it does not seem convenient for us.

There is a reason why Jesus made the statements that He made about forgiveness. The simple truth is that real faith cannot operate in an unforgiving heart, because an unforgiving heart denies the grace of God.

A person who refuses to forgive lacks the confidence necessary to appropriate the promises of God's Word. A refusal to forgive will not prevent you from being healed, but it will prevent your faith from working the way that it should—and healing comes by faith. The heart is the same place that we are to believe; according to Romans 10:9, we are to believe in our hearts.

Simply put, an unforgiving heart is an unbelieving heart. When you refuse to forgive someone, that person becomes an idol to you. You cannot place 100 percent confidence in God when idols are blocking your heart.

FORGIVENESS AND LOVE

Faith works by love according to Galatians 5:6. The word for "worketh" there is the Greek word *energeo*, which means "to be operative" (Strong, G1754). In other words, love (*agape* in Galatians 5:6) is the force by which our faith works. Without it, real faith is not able to operate. As a matter of fact, a refusal to forgive a person is an indictment against our relationship with God. It means that we do not really trust His Word.

The Bible says that if you "forgive not men their trespasses, neither will your Father forgive your trespasses" (Matt. 6:15). This means that you will remain in the prison you have created for yourself through unforgiveness.

We have seen this sort of thing a million times: believers unable to stand firm in their faith because they have resentment and bitterness in their hearts. This is strictly prohibited in the Scripture. We must remember that faith is not just an expectation of something good from God, but it is a holistic confidence and trust in the authority and absoluteness of God.

Real faith is always demonstrated through our obedience. Without obedience to the Word of God, what we call faith may instead be religious jargon. We cannot say we trust God for our healing when we are walking around resenting people. It is important for our hearts to be clean when we stand on the Word, because standing on the Word requires perseverance. It is true that many people use the issue of unforgiveness to condemn people by saying things like, "The reason you are sick is because you are bitter." I personally believe that we can use more wisdom in areas such as this.

As we will see shortly, there are certain diseases that can be directly attributed to unforgiveness, because unforgiveness was the sin that opened the door to a specific spirit of affliction. In other words, it produced the atmosphere that empowered the work of that particular demon.

Oftentimes, God will give a word of knowledge in such situations. However, we must realize that this is not always the issue. There are times when people are unaware that they are in unforgiveness, and God will still heal them as an act of His grace and mercy. But, when we are knowingly and willingly refusing to forgive someone who hurt or wounded us, we are involved in willful sin that can damage our faith walk.

RESENTMENT PRODUCES DARKNESS

John wrote: "He that saith he is in the light, and hateth his brother, is in darkness even until now" (1 John 2:9). The Bible tells us very clearly that if we hate someone, we are actually abiding in darkness.

What does this have to do with forgiveness? Well, first of all we must define what the apostle John is referring to when he says "hateth." To hate is to detest or have a strong dislike for someone. The Bible says that if we hate a brother or sister, we are actually abiding in darkness.

Remember that faith is based on the truth of God's Word. The light always represents truth and revelation in the Scriptures. God abides in truth. Darkness represents deception and sin. The Word of God says that if we are knowingly resenting someone, we are actually operating in deception. This deception tells us that we are trusting God when in fact we are not.

Darkness also represents satanic activity. It is the place where demons dwell. Demons have the legal right to operate in the dark. Earlier I mentioned that there are some specific afflictions directly related to unforgiveness: this is true and scriptural. It is powerfully illustrated in a parable in Matthew 18:

> *Then came Peter to him, and said, Lord, how oft shall my brother sin against me, and I forgive him? till seven times? Jesus saith unto him, I say not unto thee, Until seven times: but, Until seventy times seven. Therefore is the kingdom of heaven likened unto a certain king, which would take account of his servants. And when he had begun to reckon, one was brought unto him, which owed him ten thousand talents. But forasmuch as he had not to pay, his lord commanded him to be sold, and his wife, and children, and all that he had, and payment to be made. The servant therefore fell down, and worshipped him, saying, Lord, have patience with me, and I will pay thee all. Then the*

lord of that servant was moved with compassion, and loosed him, and forgave him the debt. But the same servant went out, and found one of his fellowservants, which owed him an hundred pence: and he laid hands on him, and took him by the throat, saying, Pay me that thou owest. And his fellowservant fell down at his feet, and besought him, saying, Have patience with me, and I will pay thee all. And he would not: but went and cast him into prison, till he should pay the debt. So when his fellowservants saw what was done, they were very sorry, and came and told unto their lord all that was done. Then his lord, after that he had called him, said unto him, O thou wicked servant, I forgave thee all that debt, because thou desiredst me: Shouldest not thou also have had compassion on thy fellowservant, even as I had pity on thee? And his lord was wroth, and delivered him to the tormentors, till he should pay all that was due unto him. So likewise shall my heavenly Father do also unto you, if ye from your hearts forgive not every one his brother their trespasses (Matthew 18:21-35).

This parable is the perfect illustration of the consequences of harboring unforgiveness toward people for any reason. Here the servant owed a debt that was impossible to pay. He sought mercy from his lord in the form of an extension of time. He asked the lord for more time to pay his debt. Instead of extending the servant more time, the lord actually canceled his debt completely.

The servant in turn went and demanded immediate payment from someone who owed him money. When the man could not pay, the servant threw him in prison. This is the nature of unforgiveness: it defies God's grace. The servant did not realize that his debt had been forgiven, so he became a debt collector.

As a result, the servant was delivered to the tormentors. The word translated "tormentor" literally means "torturer" (Strong, G930). A torturer is someone who puts a prisoner through excruciating pain.

Some people might say, "I am under grace. This warning does not apply to me." Beloved, there is a difference between God's grace being available to us and our being under it. The evidence that you and I have received grace is that we are able to extend it. The man in this parable had not truly received God's grace and mercy. Therefore he was unable to grant mercy to his fellow servant.

What does all of this have to do with healing and forgiveness? His refusal to forgive opened the door for him to be tormented by demonic spirits. This is what the apostle John is referring to when he talks about walking in darkness. When we are in hatred, we have opened the door for spiritual darkness.

Many demon spirits take advantage of such opportunities to afflict people physically. Some physical ailments have a direct correlation with unforgiveness. These include hypertension, osteoarthritis, gout, and stroke, to name a few.

As I mentioned before, our faith to appropriate God's Word is unable to function in the environment of darkness. By resenting those who have wounded us, we give Satan the right to torment us unnecessarily. Again, a refusal to forgive will not prevent anyone from being healed, but it will definitely open the door to satanic oppression.

TESTIMONY: LETTING IN THE ENEMY

A couple of years ago I noticed pain and stiffness in my legs that was present every morning when I woke up to pray. I would pray about it and it would go away temporarily. After this persisted for several months, I sought the Lord about it. I asked Him why this thing was bothering me like this, when I believed I walk in divine health.

As I continued to seek the Lord, He gave me a word of knowledge: "anger." I asked the Lord what that had to do with my joints. He revealed to me that anger had settled in my joints. I asked Him to show me the root cause of the anger, and He did. My work environment at the time was very stressful, and I was receiving a lot of mistreatment. I was angry with my coworkers and superiors and did not even realize it. I repented of my resentment toward them and the pain subsided. I have not had any problems since then.

The point of this testimony is to show you how I had allowed the enemy in. I gave that spirit of infirmity a suitable dwelling place by harboring resentment and refusing to forgive. I was walking in darkness and didn't even know it, so I was unable to exercise authority over it. I did not even see where it was coming from.

This is the danger of unforgiveness. God's will is for us to be well. He wants us to be healthy, both physically and spiritually. God does not want us to be distracted with resentment toward people. We must walk by faith, and the only way to do that is to put absolute trust and confidence in Him. When we are angry with people, we are placing our confidence in them.

This is a faith issue. Every blessing and promise in the Word of God is obtained by faith. Faith works by love; the more we walk in love, the more our faith works. If we are not walking in love, our faith is inoperative.

This is not to condemn anyone who has been wounded or hurt in the past. This is not to say, "You are sick because you are mad at someone." God is a God of mercy and compassion. He wants you to receive the fullness of all He has. God's fullness dwells in the light, where He dwells.

If we are to receive the fullness of God, we too must walk in the light. Remember: the act of forgiving someone in itself is an act of faith based, not on our ability, but on His grace.

POWER IN PRAYER

Father in the name of Jesus Christ, I thank You for the blood of Jesus that was shed on the cross for my sins. I thank You for the work of redemption that brought about my healing according to First Peter

2:24. I freely forgive all those who have wounded or offended me. I release all my debtors as an act of my free will. Lord, through Your grace I receive complete restoration in Jesus' name. Amen.

CHAPTER 12

It's Already Done!

For we which have believed do enter into rest, as he said, As I have sworn in my wrath, if they shall enter into my rest: although the works were finished from the foundation of the world (Hebrews 4:3).

As we examine the subject of healing, it is important for us to understand what has been accomplished for us. We stated in earlier chapters that our faith relationship with God is based on the authority of the Word of God. We must understand *why* we have a right to be healed. The simple truth is that Jesus paid the price for our healing. He was the one who conquered sin and sickness on the cross two thousand years ago.

Many people never appropriate healing because they base their healing on their own ability and not on the finished work of the cross. The Bible says in Hebrews 4 that the works were finished from the foundation of the world. In other words, the atoning work of Jesus Christ was already completed. We are admonished by the Word of God to enter into the finished work. God did everything that He was going to do for us in Christ.

Ephesians chapter 1 declares that God has already blessed us with all spiritual blessings in Christ. This means that healing is not something that God will do for us; it is in fact something that He has already done. It is amazing to think about the fact that my healing is a done deal.

A COMPLETELY FINISHED WORK

Years ago, when I attended university, I studied computer science. As a first-year student, I learned about a principle called encapsulation. This is a theory that involves a programmer hiding the contents of one program within another program or object.

This is similar to what took place on the cross. Our healing was contained within the finished work of Christ. It is not a separate work outside of our salvation, but it is encapsulated within the atonement. When we think about healing in that context, it forever changes the way we approach healing. It takes the pressure off my own goodness as the commodity that produces healing; it becomes God and God alone.

When the Bible says that the work is finished, it means exactly that. Too many in the Body of Christ are being afflicted and even dying unnecessarily, because they do not understand this simple truth: Jesus paid it all. There is no more debt to be paid. There are no unresolved accounts in heaven.

Some may say, "Well I have to do something, don't I?" Yes! You must believe.

Belief is more than saying the right things. Believing involves acting on what you accept as being true. Many people say they believe God to be their Healer, but when things do not go the way they expect, they don't act in ways that reflect their claims. When we accept the finished work of Christ in our lives, we are at rest. We are not worried or in turmoil, but we have peace. The absence of peace indicates unbelief! Though we may argue that we believe, our actions will be the true measuring stick of what we say.

So many Christians are attempting to muster up enough faith to produce their healing. This is a mistake. Christ already died for us. He already took the penalty for our sins and positioned us favorably with God the Father through His atoning blood. The Bible says in Hebrews 11:6:

> *But without faith it is impossible to please him: for he that cometh to God must believe that he is, and that he is a rewarder of them that diligently seek him.*

In short, we must believe that God is exactly who He says He is. When we place our confidence in God and have an authentic revelation of who He is, we are depending on His ability, and not our own.

"ARREST" THE CRIMINAL

Divine health is a spiritual reality based on legal authority. It is your legal right to walk in healing. Now, consider this parallel: Civil and criminal laws protect your personal space as an individual. If you were being harassed on your job by a coworker, you would tell the offender to cease the inappropriate behavior. If the behavior continued, you would have the right to take action by reporting the violation to management. Why? Because the behavior is a violation of the law.

Healing is no different. It belongs to the born-again believer by virtue of their inheritance in Christ. Sickness is an infringement upon the believer's right to be well in Jesus' name. When a criminal (the enemy) seeks to impede my God-ordained rights, he must be stopped immediately.

One common misperception is that God allows some sicknesses, as if He and the devil partner on certain things. Jesus said that Satan was a murderer from the beginning, and referred to him as the father of lies (see John 8:44). Satan is a wicked and rebellious spirit that hates God and His children.

Satan seeks to steal, kill, and destroy, but Christ came that we might have life and have it more abundantly (see John 10:10). When a thief tries to break into your house the only action to take is to stop him in his tracks. Sickness is a trespasser. It does not have the legal right to reside in the body of a believer. Like many things, however, if we do not know our rights, we cannot enforce them.

We must see sickness for what it really is: an unauthorized criminal. Many people in the Body of Christ don't see sickness this way, and therein lies much of the problem. If we don't recognize sickness as the sinister lawbreaker it is, we will tolerate it. Whatever we tolerate will dominate us.

I realize that seeing sickness and disease this way doesn't come naturally to every believer: this line of thought only comes from knowing what the Word of God says. The more we study God's Word, the more we will see things from His point of view.

RENEW YOUR MIND

Realizing that Christ already conquered sickness on the cross, and treating our bodies accordingly, requires mind renewal. We have to cultivate the "already done" mindset. It does not matter how intimidating the sickness or disease is, or how much the devil tells us that we will never get well. *It is already done!* Jesus gave us His best on the cross, and the devil's best is no match for it.

Let us take a few moments and think about the concept of something already being completed. The Bible says this:

> When Jesus therefore had received the vinegar, he said, **It is finished:** and he bowed his head, and gave up the ghost (John 19:30).

Jesus declared that it was finished. The Greek word translated "finished" here is the word *teleo*, which means "to bring to a close, to finish, to end" (Strong, G5055). It denotes a full payment for something to the extent that there is no more to be paid. It represents a period of time or a season that has come to an end. In other words, Jesus paid the price and thus brought our season of judgment and oppression to a close. Christ ended Satan's reign in our lives, once and for all.

So, do we really believe that it is finished? If we do, it will drastically change how we approach healing. We will realize that Christ already did everything that needed to be done. We will not need to focus on our strength or our goodness—we will rely on what He did.

The next time you or anyone you know is physically afflicted, I want you to close your eyes and imagine the finished work of the cross. I want you to imagine that affliction being nailed to the cross and being put to death with Jesus. Then I want you to declare that the disease is a defeated foe. It has no more power to afflict pain on you.

You already have the victory over sickness in Jesus' name!

POWER IN PRAYER

Thank You, Father, for the truths Your Word reveals about Christ's finished work! Thank You for the reality of the cross and all that was accomplished by Jesus on my behalf. Thank You for revealing the riches of this grace more and more each day, so that I would walk in the fullness of it, and share it with others. I receive every gift that Jesus purchased for me. In His precious name. Amen.

CHAPTER 13

Possessing Your Healing

*For a testament is of force after men are
dead: otherwise it is of no strength at all
while the testator liveth* (Hebrews 9:17).

The bottom line in all of this is that we must *place a demand*
on the promises of God's Word. Healing is something that
we have to *take possession of.*

Hebrews 9:17 tells us that a covenant is enforced after
someone dies. In other words, Jesus died on the cross and
thereby ratified the New Covenant in His own blood. His
shed blood gives us the legal right to inherit the benefits
and blessings of the New Covenant.

The blood covenant is important to understand. It is a
seal and assurance of specific and tangible guarantees. We
are in fact covenant children of God entitled to a specific
and tangible inheritance as a result of the New Covenant. We are the ones tasked with appropriating the New

Covenant. If we do not appropriate it in faith, we will not see its manifestation in our lives.

IT IS NOT GOD'S FAULT

Many people complain about the circumstances of their lives. Many are angry and frustrated about sickness in their bodies—but it is not God's fault. God abolished the work of Satan through Christ's work on the cross. In fact, God has done everything that He is going to do concerning our healing. Now we must place a demand on the Word of God in order to see it manifested in our lives.

This book was not written for passive believers. It is not intended for people who want to throw pity parties or blame someone else for their pain. This book speaks to those who want God's best for their lives.

Several years ago, I was in a place where I thought sickness was normal. I saw so much of it that I came to accept it. I knew more Christians who were sick than people in the world. When I reflect back on where I was in my mind, I realize what a disturbing place it was.

While I was in that place, I realized that what I was seeing was not the will of God for my life. As a matter of fact, I remember when I met my wife; she struggled with migraine headaches. One day we were together and she complained of pain in her head. I went to her almost unconsciously and said, "Peace be still. You are healed in Jesus' name."

Instantly the headache went away. She has never had that struggle since. Little did I know that God was seeding

Pesce be steal

our ministry of healing and deliverance. Like most of you reading this book, I realized that there had to be more to being a Christian than singing songs and going to church. There was a life of healing and wholeness. God wants us whole; we have to possess the wholeness that God made available to us in Christ.

This understanding has changed my life and the lives of those around me. Sickness is not normal, nor is it something we should accept. The Word of God is true, and it works every time. We have to come to a place where we are ready to take possession of wholeness.

AUTHORITY AND POWER

Jesus declared: "Behold, I give you power to tread on serpents and scorpions, and over all the power of the enemy: and nothing shall by any means hurt you" (Luke 10:19). This scripture tells us exactly what God intended in the life of a believer. He intended for us to take authority over the enemy.

The first word translated "power" in this passage is the Greek word *exousia*. It means "power of choice," and the "power of authority." We dealt with this word in Chapter 4. God has given us authority. We are to exercise this authority over all the power of the enemy. The second word translated "power" is used to describe Satan's ability. It is the word *dynamis* (or *dunamis*), which means "strength" or "ability."

This is a very important concept to understand. Satan has power, but you have authority. Your authority means that the right or control has been delegated to you and can be enforced by a system greater than you. In other words, because God gave you the authority, He stands behind it.

Imagine for a second, a police officer: A police officer has a gun, which is a form of power. The gun can harm others, therefore it can also motivate action. The gun represents *dynamis*.

However, giving a police officer a gun is not enough. The officer must also carry a badge. The badge represents the officer's legal right to exercise power. It signifies the greater authority that backs the officer's actions. This is why people ask for the officer's badge number—it accesses the authority or government that officer represents. The badge is the idea behind *exousia*. Authority is our heavenly badge or signet that gives us the legal right to tell the devil where to sit.

Criminals might carry guns, but only licensed officers have badges. In the same way, demons have power to do various things, but only a born-again, blood-washed believer has been given the spiritual authority backed by God. Notice I said *the authority,* because there is only one authority: the name above every name, "that at the name of Jesus, every knee should bow... [and] every tongue should confess that Jesus Christ is Lord..." (Phil. 2:10-11). Sickness and disease must bow to the authority vested in us by the name of Jesus.

Imagine for a moment that you are a wealthy businessperson who has one son. Imagine also that you have accumulated tremendous wealth and resources and have turned it all over to him. Then you leave the country for a year. When you return, you find your son living out of a garbage can.

How would you feel? You would be frustrated to discover that all the time and sacrifice you put into providing a quality life for your child did not have the effect you intended. Instead of taking advantage of your provision, your son was living beneath his means and potential.

I think God often feels the same way. He has given us so much. He gave His only begotten Son so that we could live in victory. Why would we live beneath the will of God for our lives?

LEARNING TO POSSESS THE PROMISES

The first thing we have to do is become convinced that healing is the children's bread. The second thing that we must do is come to the revelation that it has already been accomplished for us on the cross. Lastly, we must take the initiative and appropriate the Word of God in our bodies.

To possess something means to take ownership over it. This is the idea in John chapter 1 when it says, "As many as received him, to them gave he power..." (John 1:12). The word in that passage is *lambano*. We saw this word earlier; it literally means to possess or "to take." In other words, you and I have to take possession of what God has already provided. The work is complete, but we must receive the fullness of the work.

To help you understand this principle I will share with you an illustration. A man had two sons: one was financially well-established and well-educated; the other was a college a dropout and gambler. The father was very old and dying, so he called his two sons and asked them what he should leave for them.

The elder, more established son said, "Father, leave me a few hundred thousand, for I am already established and concerned only about your well-being."

The other son asked for all of his debt to be paid off.

The father willed each of the sons a portion of his inheritance. The first son was given $100,000 in the will. The second was given a key with instructions attached to it. The instructions directed the son to drive ninety minutes to a certain building at 9:00 A.M.

The son replied with amusement and said, "What is this? I asked for money to pay my debt."

He took the key and left puzzled. The night before he was scheduled to visit the building, he went to the casino and gambled all night long. Predictably, he overslept and awakened at 10:00 A.M. No sooner did he realize it was too late to keep the appointment, that he forgot about the whole thing and went to breakfast.

Later that day, he received a phone call telling him that, because he missed his appointment, the safety deposit box was no longer available. He asked what was in the box, and the man on the phone said, "One hundred million dollars."

The son dropped to the floor and wept.

The point of the illustration is that this is how most of the Church has behaved. The Father has left us an inheritance which is more than sufficient to pay every debt in our lives. He literally paid it all. But like the younger son, many of us have failed to take possession of what he has given us.

We must put pressure on the promises of God. His Word is like the safety deposit box in the story. In it is everything that we need and more. But, even though it is full of resources, it means very little unless we unlock it.

HIS AUTHORITY IN US

When we combine an understanding of the finished work of Christ, with an understanding of the authority of the name of Jesus, sickness must evacuate every area of our lives. It is not about any authority; it is about *His* authority that lives in us.

The Scripture declares that "greater is he that is in you, than he that is in the world" (1 John 4:4). We have been given authority over all the power of the enemy, including all sickness and disease. It is authority over anything the devil inflicts upon our lives.

God has called us to tread on sickness and disease. He wants us to trample multiple sclerosis. He wants us to put heart disease under our feet.

Then the Word of God declares that "nothing shall by any means hurt you" (Luke 10:19). This is a profound revelation. In the original Greek, the Word of God is saying that nothing the devil has available can violate or damage the law God has established. Satan's kingdom has to operate within the confines of God's law. Therefore, anytime Satan afflicts a born-again believer with sickness, he is breaking the law, and you and I have been given *exousia* (authority) by God to stop him.

We are not supposed to be afraid of the devil. We are not supposed to bow to any evil report. Too many in the Body of Christ have treated Satan as if he were God's equal. He is not equal; there is none higher than the Most High God.

We must possess what God has provided in Christ. We must decide that we will give the devil no place in our lives. One of the biggest deceptions of Satan is to get us to tolerate sickness, because he knows that whatever we tolerate he will in turn use to dominate us. I repeat, give him no place.

What if I told you that you could walk in divine health? What if I told you that you could be 100 percent healed, never to be bound with that affliction again? Do you believe that?

It is as simple as accepting the sovereignty of God in redeeming your total being. You must make up your mind that God is bigger than everything else.

POWER IN PRAYER

I urge you to repeatedly and confidently say this prayer aloud:

Father, in the name of Jesus Christ, I thank You that, because of Christ's blood, You hear me. Thank You, Father, that I am healed completely through the atoning work of Jesus Christ on the cross. Every area of my body must submit to the Lordship of Jesus. Every cell in my body functions perfectly. Every atom in my body is under Your control and authority. I am healed and whole in the name of Jesus. First Peter 2:24 declares that I have been healed by His stripes. I am healed in Jesus' name. I walk in the divine health that You have ordained for my life. Thank You, Jesus Christ, for being my Healer. I release any and all offenses in my heart that would hinder my faith from operating the way that it should. Thank You, Lord, for Your grace! In Jesus' name. Amen.

The following prayer addresses specific diseases:

Father, in the name of Jesus Christ; I now appropriate the Word of God contained in Your Book and in this book as an act of my free will. I declare that my body is a vessel of honor, and the temple of the Holy Spirit. I now take dominion over this body and command the following diseases, symptoms, and/or afflictions to cease operation: autoimmune disorder, multiple sclerosis, diabetes, lupus, cancer (prostate, lung, cervical, skin, brain, etc.), leukemia, high blood pressure, insulin resistance, thyroid disorder, preeclampsia, depression (postpartum, etc.), heart diseases, arthritis, osteoporosis, sickle cell, hemophilia, viral infections, bacterial infections, meningitis, protein disorders, and any other symptom, abnormality, virus, affliction, or disease. I am totally healed through the shed blood of

CALSEIUM DISORDER

Jesus Christ. Thank You, Lord, for my healing! In the name of Jesus Christ, I pray. Amen.

CHAPTER 14

Sacred Cows

As a pastor, I have come across countless people and circumstances that reveal the thoughts and beliefs people have about God, His nature, and the way He deals with His creation.

Unfortunately, religion has done much damage to the way people perceive God. As a matter of fact, in the past several years I have had to invest more time and energy to minister healing and deliverance to people in the Church than people outside of the Church.

One reason for this is the fact that many in the Church have been taught to believe in certain unbiblical ways. These ways are what I refer to as "sacred cows." For the purpose of this book, a sacred cow is a way of thinking or believing that has to some degree been held sacred or untouchable. In other words, it is believed *because it is believed*.

CONDITIONED BELIEF SYSTEMS

To illustrate this idea, I want to share with you a story about things people believe. Several years ago, an experiment was performed on monkeys to illustrate the power of classical conditioning. In the experiment, researchers took five monkeys and placed them in a cage. In the center of the cage was a ladder. Above the ladder, on the ceiling, a banana was attached to a string.

Once left to their own devices, the monkeys rushed to climb the ladder and grab the banana. When the first monkey reached the prize, the researchers sprayed the monkey with a powerful water hose.

This pattern repeated itself until that monkey gave up, and another monkey tried for the banana.

This time, the researchers changed their approach: Instead of spraying the monkey that climbed the ladder, they sprayed the other monkeys. Each time one monkey mounted the ladder, the other monkeys were sprayed.

After several repetitions of this pattern, the researchers removed one of the original monkeys that had climbed the ladder, and replaced him with a new monkey. This animal had never been in community with the rest of the group. Immediately, he tried to get the banana, and immediately he met with a vicious attack from the other monkeys.

The researchers then removed another of the original monkeys and replaced it with a second new one. The second newcomer saw the banana and went for it, only to be coached by his immediate predecessor. The first "new" monkey confided, "We don't touch the banana."

The second "new" monkey asked, "Why not?"

His first newcomer said, "Because it has always been that way."

The first new monkey had no idea how things had always been. He only knew that his first attempt at the banana was met with opposition. He assumed it had "always been" that way.

There are many unscriptural beliefs held in the Church. Many of them have prevented Christians from relating to God properly, and from receiving what God has for them. These sacred cows are detrimental; therefore, I want to specifically address several of them. (This is by no means an exhaustive list.)

Sacred Cow #1: It Is Not God's Will to Heal Everybody.

One of the most disturbing and widely held beliefs that I find in the Church is the notion that healing is not for everyone.

In other words, God may heal some people, but not others. Beloved, this is not biblical. I repeat: this is not a biblical belief system. One of my favorite books of the Bible is the Gospel of Luke. Luke's Gospel has more accounts of healing than any other book of the Bible. The amazing thing is that, in the book of Luke, Jesus never turned down a single person who asked for healing.

If Jesus were in the business of healing some people and not others, then surely He would have told some of them, "I cannot heal you, for it is not the Father's will."

However, the Bible says this in Luke 6:19: "And the whole multitude sought to touch him: for there went virtue out of Him and healed them all."

The interesting thing about this account is that the writer used the Greek word *ochlos,* which denotes a crowd or troop of people—"a throng"—gathered together (Strong, G3793). This definition also distinguishes common people from the ruling class. This is very significant because it helps us to have a picture of the heart of God concerning healing. He did not heal a special category of people; He healed the crowd, a multitude of people. In other words, He did not discriminate in His healing.

If this were not enough to convince us, Luke added that Jesus "healed them all." In the original Greek, the word *pas* is used. It is literally translated "each, every, any, all, the whole..." (Strong, G3956). We can see that God wants to make clear that everyone who came to Him was healed.

Recently, I saw a gentleman on television assert that there were some people whom Jesus did not heal. Unfortunately, he must have read a Bible no one else has ever seen, because that statement was absolutely incorrect. There is not one person in the New Testament whom Jesus did not heal.

There was one thing that inhibited Jesus' work: The Bible explains:

> *He could there do no mighty work, save that he laid his hands upon a few sick folk, and healed them. And he marvelled **because of their unbelief** (Mark 6:5-6).*

In this account, we see that the only thing that limited Christ's healing power was unbelief. Even in this example, there were still people that He laid hands on, and the ones who were prayed for were healed. The truth of the matter is that Christ always manifested healing to all those who would receive it. There is no reason for anyone to teach or believe that God will only heal certain people at certain times and not heal everyone. Do not buy into the lie that is designed to rob you of what God has provided.

Sacred Cow #2: Healing Is Not Available Today

Though this is better classified as a lie rather than a sacred cow, I included it because of the surprising number of people who believe it. I have heard countless arguments proclaiming that healing gifts are not in operation anymore. I even had a conversation with a man in a Christian bookstore. The man had difficulty believing in healing. He told me he was very skeptical of "stuff like that." Ironically, "stuff like that" was the foundation of the early Church, as well as Jesus' ministry on Earth.

Here is what Luke 4:18-19 says:

> *The spirit of the Lord is upon me, because he hath anointed me to preach the gospel to the poor; he hath sent me to heal the brokenhearted, to preach deliverance to captives, and recovering of sight to the blind, to set at liberty them that are bruised, to preach the acceptable year of the Lord.*

This passage reveals the things that Jesus was sent by God to do. One of those things is to heal the brokenhearted. The word used for "heal" in this case is the Greek work *iaomai*. The word means "to cure, heal; to make whole."

The context of this passage is salvation or deliverance. We know that Luke was referring to physical healing for two reasons: (1) The word translated "brokenhearted" literally means "to tear one's body" (Strong, G4937). So we understand that being brokenhearted is not just an emotional thing in this text. It literally means to be physically oppressed by Satan. (2) Jesus confirmed that this is true by physically healing the sick. If it were an emotional healing only, He would only have addressed people's emotional states. He did not. Jesus was both a physical and spiritual Healer. He came to liberate people from their captivity to sin, and from physical oppression.

Another example supporting the availability of healing is found in Luke 13:11-13:

> *And, behold, there was a woman which had a spirit of infirmity eighteen years, and was bowed together, and could in no wise lift up herself. And when Jesus saw her, he called her to him, and said unto her, Woman, thou art loosed from thine infirmity. And he laid his hand on her: and immediately she was made straight, and glorified God.*

Here we see another display of the miraculous power of God. This is a manifestation of God's healing plan. I love the verbiage used in this passage: "immediately she was made straight." She had literally been deformed and contorted by Satan himself. She was bound under satanic power that removed her from God's original intent for her life. Jesus literally put her back the way she was supposed to be. She was one of the brokenhearted that Jesus came to heal.

Jesus has the power to put us back together again!

The point of these illustrations is to demonstrate that healing was more than the isolated acts of Jesus as the Son of God. Every healing miracle in the Scripture was a manifestation of God's plan to heal His creation and make it whole.

Those who believe that healing is no longer in operation are asserting that the plan of God for His creation has somehow changed. It hasn't. God's plan for healing and restoration is alive and well today. God tells us in Malachi 3:6: "I am the LORD, I change not...."

God has not changed. The Bible says that He is the same yesterday, today, and forever (see Heb. 13:8). This biblical truth is further illustrated in Mark 16:17-18:

> *And these signs shall follow them that believe; in my name shall they cast out devils; they shall speak with new tongues; they shall take up serpents; and if they drink any deadly thing, it shall not hurt them; they shall lay hands on the sick, and they shall recover.*

Here we see that Jesus gives clear and distinct instructions to His disciples. He describes how we should operate after His ascension. The phrase "they shall lay hands" is written in the active voice, which means it is something that we were charged with doing and performing continuously.

We are responsible for walking in this reality. The phrase "they shall" at the end of verse 18 is telling. In the Greek "they shall" is the word *echo,* and this word means "to own" or "possess" (Strong, G2192). In other words, we must take ownership over this truth; we must possess it. It is a promise, a guarantee. If we are believers and we lay hands on the sick, the Word of God declares that they shall recover. They absolutely, positively shall.

It does not sound to me like healing is no longer in operation. In fact, the early Church was established by the miraculous and continues to manifest the miraculous today. Remember that Jesus is alive. If His arm is so short that He cannot physically heal, how then can we claim that He can save a hell-bound sinner, which is clearly a greater miracle?

The simple truth is that the healing plan of God is just as firm as it was when Christ walked the earth. Besides all this, there is not a single scripture in the Bible that says healing went "out of business."

Religion can be a very dangerous thing. Beloved, I have endeavored to base my theology on the uncompromised Word of God.

Sacred Cow #3: God Uses Sickness to Teach Us a Lesson!

This is probably the most widely held and commonly proclaimed sacred cow in the Church today. As a matter of fact, this is a sacred cow that I personally held for a large portion of my Christian experience. Whether this belief is conscious or subconscious, it has probably affected all of us at one point or another. It is affecting many in the Body of Christ right now.

Earlier in this book, we dealt with the temptation to mischaracterize God. It is critical to understand the dangers of such mischaracterization. For most of my life I thought God was waiting to punish me at any moment.

I saw Him as always seeking to make me pay for some wrong that I had done. This belief was rooted in legalism. Unfortunately, for me, I transferred this way of thinking over to my Christian life.

This mindset is often empowered through false teaching. It stems from an Old Covenant way of thinking. A while ago, I heard a pastor say that the reason why one of his members was admitted into the hospital was because "God was trying to teach him something."

Although I believe in the sovereignty of God; I also know from scripture that God's sovereignty has boundaries. The Word of God declares in Psalms 138:2: "thou hast magnified thy word above all thy name." Here we see that the sovereignty of God is expressed through His Word. The notion of God's sovereignty outside of the confines of His Word is unbiblical at best.

The truth is that God does not use sickness to teach a born-again believer anything, no more than you, as a parent would break your child's arm to teach him or her a lesson.

Some may say, "But I am not God." Well, the Bible says this: "If ye then, being evil, know how to give good gifts unto your children, how much more shall your Father which is heaven give good things to them that ask him?" (Matt. 7:11).

The word for "evil" here is the word *ponēros*, which means "of a bad nature" (Strong, G4190). It is used to illustrate the fact that even with a bad nature, human beings inherently desire to do good things for their children. How much more does a good-natured God want to do well by His children?

When that pastor talked about his parishioner being sick at the hand of God, it broke my heart. So, although it is right to assert that we are not God, it only serves as further proof of the error in believing that God would use sickness to teach us.

The book of Genesis tells us that we are made in the very image of God (see Gen. 1:26-27). This means that He has placed in us identification with His nature. This is why even the worst sinner is angered by the death of a child. Justice is absolute and universally embraced by every human being, *because* all of us were made in God's image.

If giving our children harmful medicine is unfathomable to us as natural parents, how could we possibly believe such cruelty of our heavenly Father? This is exactly what people are suggesting when they say, "God is using this cancer to teach me," or "He's testing me."

The Bible makes it clear that God cannot be tempted with evil, and does not tempt us (see James 1:13). When was the last time you learned a valuable lesson from being sick? The only lesson I have ever learned from being sick is that I hate sickness and never want to be sick again. Besides, if God orchestrated a test to show you something, you would never pass it!

The only thing that is tested for believers is their faith. Scripture says: "Knowing this, that the trying of your faith worketh patience" (James 1:3). God allows our faith to be tried because it produces endurance. God wants our faith to be strong because our faith pleases Him. Our faith is tested by circumstances to prove its authenticity. This is totally different from God making a believer sick.

Sacred Cow #4: Sickness Is My Thorn in the Flesh

This is one of my favorite sacred cows because, like the notion that God uses sickness to teach us, this is a widely held belief. I have said before and will continue to affirm that our faith must be based on the Word of God. In addition, we must rightly divide His Word (see 2 Tim. 2:15). This idea really hits home for me because I have had people whom I greatly respect and trust use this verse completely out of context.

In the book of Second Corinthians Paul shared his dilemma. He defended his apostleship and shared his encounters with visions and revelations from God.

Notice what Paul said:

> *And lest I should be exalted above measure through the abundance of the revelations, there was given to me a thorn in the flesh, the messenger of Satan to buffet me, lest I should be exalted above measure* (2 Corinthians 12:7).

To understand the insidious nature of this sacred cow, we must closely examine this passage and clearly understand what it is saying. The Greek word *hyperairō* is used to describe being exalted. This exaltation is what will happen in the absence of the "thorn in the flesh." The word translated "exalted" is not necessarily used in a negative sense. It means "to lift or raise up over some thing" (Strong, G5229).

In essence Paul said the thorn kept him from being "lifted above measure, through the abundance of revelation."

The thing to seriously note here is that somehow, this has been represented to mean that God was trying to keep Paul humble by doing something bad to him. Unfortunately, this is nowhere stated or implied in the text. Think about this for a second: Would God punish His ministers for knowing too much about Him? That doesn't make any sense! God knows how much revelation we can handle. Would He give us more than we can handle and then punish us so that we don't become prideful? This is clearly an incorrect train of thought.

This is what the Bible says:

> *That the God of our Lord Jesus Christ, the Father of glory, may give unto you the spirit of wisdom and revelation in the knowledge of him...* (Ephesians 1:17).

It is the pleasure of God for us to have revelation about Him. For years I would use this passage out of context, because of how I was taught. God is not in the business of playing games with us. We serve a very consistent and compassionate God who longs to reveal Himself to us.

The second dimension to this sacred cow is the fact that there is no mention of sickness at all. Sickness is in no way referenced as a thorn. The word translated "thorn" in this passage literally means a "pointed piece of wood...a stake" (Strong, G4647).

Paul says that a splinter was given to him. Think about this for a second. A splinter is an irritation or agitation of some sort that gets underneath the skin. It is not a good thing. Remember that every good gift is from above (see James 1:17). If Paul's thorn were from God it would be a good thing.

The third dimension of this idea is that the Bible tells us exactly where the thorn originated. Second Corinthians 12:7 tells us that it was the "messenger of Satan." The word for messenger is the Greek word *aggelos,* which refers to an angelic messenger (Strong, G32).

We see two things from this passage: (1) The thorn was a spirit. Paul's affliction was spiritual in nature. (2) We see that the spirit came from Satan himself. Satan sent a spirit to afflict or oppress Paul.

This should change our perception of the whole passage. God was not beating down Paul to teach him a lesson. This was a case of Satan oppressing Paul to prevent him from receiving more revelation. Satan does not want us to have revelation about God, because the more we know about God the more we will take authority over Satan.

We can further see the nature of this "thorn" by looking at how the apostle Paul responded to it: *"For this thing I besought the Lord thrice, that it might depart from me"* (2 Cor. 12:8). Paul asked God if the thing might depart. Interestingly, the word translated "depart" is *aphistemi.* It means "to make stand off, cause to withdraw" (Strong, G868). This is military terminology that denotes an attack. Paul asked God to cause this attack to be withdrawn. God responded, saying, "My grace is sufficient..." (2 Cor. 12:9).

God told Paul that the grace He had given him was enough to deal with whatever was coming against Him. God never said, "No, Paul I shall not deliver you." That is nowhere in the Scripture. In fact, God told the apostle that His power was all he needed.

Paul did not glory in revelations; he gloried in the fact that, when he was at his weakest, the power of Almighty God was at his disposal. In the next verse, Paul explained exactly what the thorn was: reproaches, necessities, persecutions, and distresses. We see this demonstrated throughout Paul's ministry: extreme persecution, accusations against him, and people withdrawing resources from him. Paul didn't take any of this personally because it caused Christ's power to rest on him in greater measure.

This is the essential message of this passage. Nowhere is there an implication of God making us sick to keep us from being lifted up in pride. As a matter of fact, there is no record in any of his epistles of Paul ever being sick. All we see is Paul walking in the supernatural power of God.

God's Word is His bond, and He promises His children many benefits. How we choose to view God and His Word determines our ability to walk in the fullness of His promises—for which Christ paid dearly. We must make up our minds; we must determine that we want what God wants for our lives.

Beloved, God wants us well, and the Bible proves it!

POWER IN PRAYER

Father, Your Word is not arbitrary or confusing. Your promises are forthright, and they are offered in love. Thank You for all that You desire for me. By Your grace, I seek to see You as You really are, and I take Your Word as You meant it to be understood. I renounce my "sacred cows" and choose instead to take every bit of Your Word to heart. Thank You for Your love and for Your truth. In Jesus' name. Amen.

CHAPTER 15

Healing Scriptures

This chapter contains healing scriptures from the New King James Version of the Bible. I have used them to minister healing and deliverance to countless numbers of people. Please read and be edified in your spirit by the unadulterated Word of God.

Exodus 15:26

> ...If you diligently heed the voice of the LORD your God and do what is right in His sight, give ear to His commandments and keep all His statutes, I will put none of the diseases on you which I have brought on the Egyptians. For I am the LORD who heals you.

Exodus 23:25–26

> So you shall serve the LORD your God, and He will bless your bread and your water. And I will take sickness away from the midst of you. No one shall

suffer miscarriage or be barren in your land; I will fulfill the number of your days.

Deuteronomy 7:13

And He will love you and bless you and multiply you; He will also bless the fruit of your womb and the fruit of your land, your grain and your new wine and your oil, the increase of your cattle and the offspring of your flock, in the land of which He swore to your fathers to give you.

Deuteronomy 28:1-14

Now it shall come to pass, if you diligently obey the voice of the LORD your God, to observe carefully all His commandments which I command you today, that the LORD your God will set you high above all nations of the earth. And all these blessings shall come upon you and overtake you, because you obey the voice of the LORD your God:

Blessed shall you be in the city, and blessed shall you be in the country. Blessed shall be the fruit of your body, the produce of your ground and the increase of your herds, the increase of your cattle and the offspring of your flocks. Blessed shall be your basket and your kneading bowl. Blessed shall you be when you come in, and blessed shall you be when you go out.

The LORD will cause your enemies who rise against you to be defeated before your face; they shall come out against you one way and flee before you seven ways.

The LORD *will command the blessing on you in your storehouses and in all to which you set your hand, and He will bless you in the land which the* LORD *your God is giving you.*

The LORD *will establish you as a holy people to Himself, just as He has sworn to you, if you keep the commandments of the* LORD *your God and walk in His ways. Then all peoples of the earth shall see that you are called by the name of the* LORD, *and they shall be afraid of you. And the* LORD *will grant you plenty of goods, in the fruit of your body, in the increase of your livestock, and in the produce of your ground, in the land of which the* LORD *swore to your fathers to give you. The* LORD *will open to you His good treasure, the heavens, to give the rain to your land in its season, and to bless all the work of your hand. You shall lend to many nations, but you shall not borrow. And the* LORD *will make you the head and not the tail; you shall be above only, and not be beneath, if you heed the commandments of the* LORD *your God, which I command you today, and are careful to observe them. So you shall not turn aside from any of the words which I command you this day, to the right or the left, to go after other gods to serve them.*

Deuteronomy 31:6

Be strong and of good courage, do not fear nor be afraid of them; for the LORD *your God, He is the*

One who goes with you. He will not leave you nor forsake you.

First Kings 3:14

So if you walk in My ways, to keep My statutes and My commandments, as your father David walked, then I will lengthen your days.

Psalms 23

The LORD is my shepherd; I shall not want. He makes me to lie down in green pastures; He leads me beside the still waters. He restores my soul; He leads me in the paths of righteousness for His name's sake. Yea, though I walk through the valley of the shadow of death, I will fear no evil; for You are with me; Your rod and Your staff, they comfort me. You prepare a table before me in the presence of my enemies; You anoint my head with oil; my cup runs over. Surely goodness and mercy shall follow me all the days of my life; and I will dwell in the house of the LORD forever.

Psalms 41:1-3

Blessed is he who considers the poor; the LORD will deliver him in time of trouble. The LORD will preserve him and keep him alive, and he will be blessed on the earth; You will not deliver him to the will of his enemies. The LORD will strengthen him on his bed of illness; You will sustain him on his sickbed.

Psalms 91

He who dwells in the secret place of the Most High shall abide under the shadow of the Almighty. I will say of the LORD; "He is my refuge and my fortress; my God, in Him I will trust."

Surely He shall deliver you from the snare of the fowler and from the perilous pestilence. He shall cover you with his feathers, and under His wings you shall take refuge; His truth shall be your shield and buckler. You shall not be afraid of the terror by night, nor of the arrow that flies by day, nor of the pestilence that walks in darkness, nor of the destruction that lays waste at noonday. A thousand may fall at your side, and ten thousand at your right hand; but it shall not come near you. Only with your eyes shall you look, and see the reward of the wicked.

Because you have made the LORD, who is my refuge, even the Most High, your dwelling place, no evil shall befall you, nor shall any plague come near your dwelling; for He shall give His angels charge over you, to keep you in all your ways. In their hands they shall bear you up, lest you dash your foot against a stone. You shall tread upon the lion and the cobra, the young lion and the serpent you shall trample underfoot.

Because he has set his love upon me, therefore I will deliver him; I will set him on high, because he has known My name. He shall call upon Me, and I will answer him; I will be with him in trouble; I will deliver him and honor him. With long life I will satisfy him, and show him My salvation.

Psalms 103:1-5

Bless the LORD, O my soul; and all that is within me, bless His holy name! Bless the LORD, O my soul, and forget not all His benefits: who forgives all your iniquities, who heals all your diseases, who redeems your life from destruction, who crowns you with lovingkindness and tender mercies, who satisfies your mouth with good things, so that your youth is renewed like the eagle's.

Psalms 105:37

He also brought them out with silver and gold, and there was none feeble among His tribes.

Psalms 107:19-20

Then they cried out to the LORD in their trouble, and He saved them out of their distresses. He sent His word and healed them, and delivered them from their destructions.

Psalms 118:17

I shall not die, but live, and declare the works of the LORD.

Proverbs 3:5-8

Trust in the LORD with all your heart, and lean not on your own understanding; in all your ways acknowledge Him, and He shall direct your paths. Do not be wise in your own eyes; fear the LORD and depart from evil. It will be health to your flesh, and strength to your bones.

Proverbs 4:20-22

My son, give attention to my words; incline your ear to my sayings. Do not let them depart from your eyes; keep them in the midst of your heart; for they are life to those who find them, and health to all their flesh.

Proverbs 9:10-11

The fear of the LORD is the beginning of wisdom, and the knowledge of the Holy One is understanding. For by me your days will be multiplied, and years of life will be added to you.

Proverbs 12:18

There is one who speaks like the piercings of a sword, but the tongue of the wise promotes health.

Proverbs 12:25

Anxiety in the heart of man causes depression, but a good word makes it glad.

Proverbs 14:30

A sound heart is life to the body, but envy is rotten-ness to the bones.

Proverbs 15:30

The light of the eyes rejoices the heart, and a good report makes the bones healthy.

Proverbs 16:24

Pleasant words are like a honeycomb, sweetness to the soul and health to the bones.

Proverbs 17:22

A merry heart does good, like medicine, but a broken spirit dries the bones.

Isaiah 30:15

For thus says the Lord GOD, the Holy One of Israel: "In returning and rest you shall be saved; in quiet-ness and confidence shall be your strength."

Isaiah 40:28-31

Have you not known? Have you not heard? The everlasting God, the LORD, the Creator of the ends of the earth, neither faints nor is weary. His under-standing is unsearchable. He gives power to the weak, and to those who have no might He increases strength. Even the youths shall faint and be weary, and the young men shall utterly fall, but those who wait on the LORD shall renew their strength; they shall mount up with wings like eagles, they shall run and not be weary, they shall walk and not faint.

Isaiah 41:10-18

"Fear not, for I am with you; be not dismayed, for I am your God. I will strengthen you, yes, I will help you, I will uphold you with My righteous right hand.' Behold, all those who were incensed against you shall be ashamed and disgraced; they shall be as nothing, and those who strive with you shall perish. You shall seek them and not find them— those who contended with you. Those who war against you shall be as nothing, as a nonexistent thing. For I, the LORD your God, will hold your right hand, saying to you, 'Fear not, I will help you.' Fear not, you worm Jacob, you men of Israel! I will help you," says the LORD and your Redeemer, the Holy One of Israel.

"Behold, I will make you into a new threshing sledge with sharp teeth; you shall thresh the mountains and beat them small, and make the hills like chaff. You shall winnow them, the wind shall carry them away, and the whirlwind shall scatter them; you shall rejoice in the LORD, and glory in the Holy One of Israel.

"The poor and needy seek water, but there is none, their tongues fail for thirst. I, the LORD, will hear them; I, the God of Israel, will not forsake them. I

will open rivers in desolate heights, and fountains in the midst of the valleys; I will make the wilderness a pool of water, and the dry land springs of water."

Isaiah 43:1-2

But now, thus says the LORD, who created you, O Jacob, and He who formed you, O Israel: "Fear not, for I have redeemed you; I have called you by your name; you are Mine. When you pass through the waters, I will be with you; and through the rivers, they shall not overflow you. When you walk through the fire, you shall not be burned, nor shall the flame scorch you."

Isaiah 53:4

Surely He has borne our griefs and carried our sorrows; yet we esteemed Him stricken, smitten by God, and afflicted.

Isaiah 55:10-11

For as the rain comes down, and the snow from heaven, and do not return there, but water the earth, and make it bring forth and bud, that it may give seed to the sower and bread to the eater, so shall My word be that goes forth from My mouth; it shall not return to Me void, but it shall accomplish what I please, and it shall prosper in the thing for which I sent it.

Isaiah 58:8

Then your light shall break forth like the morning, your healing shall spring forth speedily, and your righteousness shall go before you; the glory of the LORD shall be your rear guard.

Isaiah 58:10-11

If you extend your soul to the hungry and satisfy the afflicted soul, then your light shall dawn in the darkness, and your darkness shall be as the noonday. The Lord will guide you continually, and satisfy your soul in drought, and strengthen your bones; you shall be like a watered garden, and like a spring of water, whose waters do not fail.

Isaiah 61:3

To console those who mourn in Zion, to give them beauty for ashes, the oil of joy for mourning, the garment of praise for the spirit of heaviness; that they may be called trees of righteousness, the planting of the LORD, that He may be glorified.

Jeremiah 30:17

"For I will restore health to you and heal you of your wounds," says the LORD, "Because they called you an outcast saying: 'This is Zion; no one seeks her.'"

Jeremiah 33:6

Behold, I will bring it health and healing; I will heal them and reveal to them the abundance of peace and truth.

Malachi 4:2

But to you who fear My name the Sun of Righteousness shall arise with healing in His wings; and you shall go out and grow fat like stall-fed calves.

Matthew 4:23

And Jesus went about all Galilee, teaching in their synagogues, preaching the gospel of the kingdom, and healing all kinds of sickness and all kinds of disease among the people.

Matthew 8:13

Then Jesus said to the centurion, "Go your way; and as you have believed, so let it be done for you." And his servant was healed that same hour.

Matthew 8:14-15

Now when Jesus had come into Peter's house, He saw his wife's mother lying sick with a fever. So He touched her hand, and the fever left her. And she arose and served them.

Matthew 8:16-17

When evening had come, they brought to Him many who were demon-possessed. And He cast out the spirits with a word, and healed all who were sick, that it might be fulfilled which was spoken by Isaiah the prophet, saying: "He Himself took our infirmities and bore our sicknesses."

Matthew 9:2

Then behold, they brought to Him a paralytic lying on a bed. When Jesus saw their faith, He said to the paralytic, "Son, be of good cheer; your sins are forgiven you."

Matthew 9:6-7

"That you may know that the Son of Man has power on earth to forgive sins"—then He said to the paralytic, "Arise, take up your bed, and go to your house." And he arose, and departed to his house.

Matthew 9:29-30

Then He touched their eyes, saying, "According to your faith let it be to you." And their eyes were opened. And Jesus sternly warned them, saying, "See that no one knows it."

Matthew 9:32-33

As they went out, behold, they brought to Him a man, mute and demon-possessed. And when the demon was cast out, the mute spoke. And the multitudes marveled, saying, "It was never seen like this in Israel!"

Matthew 9:35

Then Jesus went about all the cities and villages, teaching in their synagogues, preaching the gospel of the kingdom, and healing every sickness and every disease among the people.

Matthew 10:1

And when He had called His twelve disciples to Him, He gave them power over unclean spirits, to cast them out, and to heal all kinds of sickness and all kinds of disease.

Matthew 10:7-8

And as you go, preach, saying, "The kingdom of heaven is at hand." Heal the sick, cleanse the lepers, raise the dead, cast out demons. Freely you have received, freely give.

Matthew 11:5

The blind see and the lame walk; the lepers are cleansed and the deaf hear; the dead are raised up and the poor have the gospel preached to them.

Matthew 12:15

But when Jesus knew it, He withdrew from there. And great multitudes followed Him, and He healed them all.

Matthew 12:17-18

That it might be fulfilled which was spoken by Isaiah the prophet, saying: "Behold! My Servant whom I have chosen, My Beloved in whom My soul is well pleased! I will put My Spirit upon Him, and He will declare justice to the Gentiles."

Matthew 14:14

And when Jesus went out He saw a great multitude; and He was moved with compassion for them, and healed their sick.

Matthew 15:28

Then Jesus answered and said to her, "O woman, great is your faith! Let it be to you as you desire." And her daughter was healed from that very hour.

Matthew 17:14-18

And when they had come to the multitude, a man came to Him, kneeling down to Him and saying, "Lord, have mercy on my son, for he is an epileptic and suffers severely; for he often falls into the fire and often into the water. So I brought him to Your disciples, but they could not cure him." Then Jesus

answered and said, "O faithless and perverse gener-
ation, how long shall I be with you? How long shall
I bear with you? Bring him here to Me." And Jesus
rebuked the demon, and it came out of him; and the
child was cured from that very hour.

Matthew 20:33-34

They said to Him, "Lord, that our eyes may be
opened." So Jesus had compassion and touched their
eyes. And immediately their eyes received sight, and
they followed Him.

Mark 1:40-41

Now a leper came to Him, imploring Him, kneel-
ing down to Him and saying to Him, "If You are
willing, You can make me clean." Then Jesus, moved
with compassion, stretched out His hand and touched
him, and said to him, "I am willing; be cleansed."

Mark 3:10

For He healed many, so that as many as had afflic-
tions pressed about Him to touch Him.

Mark 5:28-29

For she said, "If only I may touch His clothes, I shall
be made well." Immediately the fountain of her blood
was dried up, and she felt in her body that she was
healed of the affliction.

Mark 5:34

And He said to her, "Daughter, your faith has made you well. Go in peace, and be healed of your affliction."

Mark 6:12-13

So they went out and preached that people should repent. And they cast out many demons, and anointed with oil many who were sick, and healed them.

Mark 6:56

Whenever He entered, into villages, cities, or the country, they laid the sick in the marketplaces, and begged Him that they might just touch the hem of His garment. And as many as touched Him were made well.

Mark 7:32-35

Then they brought to Him one who was deaf and had an impediment in his speech, and they begged Him to put His hand on him. And He took him aside from the multitude, and put His fingers in his ears, and He spat and touched his tongue. Then, looking up to heaven, He sighed, and said to him, "Ephphatha," that is, "Be opened." Immediately his ears were opened, and the impediment of his tongue was loosed, and he spoke plainly.

Mark 10:46-52

Now they came to Jericho. As He went out of Jericho with His disciples and a great multitude, blind Bartimaeus, the son of Timaeus, sat by the road begging. And when he heard that it was Jesus of Nazareth, he began to cry out and say, "Jesus, Son of David, have mercy on me!" Then many warned him to be quiet; but he cried out all the more, "Son of David, have mercy on me!" So Jesus stood still and commanded him to be called. Then they called the blind man, saying to him, "Be of good cheer. Rise, He is calling you." And throwing aside his garment, he rose and came to Jesus. So Jesus answered and said to him, "What do you want Me to do for you?" The blind man said to Him, "Rabboni, that I may receive my sight." Then Jesus said to him, "Go your way; your faith has made you well." And immediately he received his sight and followed Jesus on the road.

Mark 16:15-18

And He said to them, "Go into all the world and preach the gospel to every creature. He who believes and is baptized will be saved; but he who does not believe will be condemned. And these signs will follow those who believe: In My name they will cast out demons; they will speak with new tongues; they will take up serpents; and if they drink anything deadly, it will by no means hurt them; they will lay hands on the sick, and they will recover."

Luke 4:40

When the sun was setting, all those who had any that were sick with various diseases brought them to Him; and He laid His hands on every one of them and healed them.

Luke 5:17

Now it happened on a certain day, as He was teaching, that there were Pharisees and teachers of the law sitting by, who had come out of every town of Galilee, Judea, and Jerusalem. And the power of the Lord was present to heal them.

Luke 6:6-10

Now it happened on another Sabbath, also, that He entered the synagogue and taught. And a man was there whose right hand was withered. So the scribes and Pharisees watched Him closely, whether He would heal on the Sabbath, that they might find an accusation against Him. But He knew their thoughts, and said to the man who had the withered hand, "Arise and stand here." And he arose and stood. Then Jesus said to them, "I will ask you one thing: Is it lawful on the Sabbath to do good or to do evil, to save life or to destroy?" And when He had looked around at them all, He said to the man,

"Stretch out your hand." And he did so, and his hand was restored as whole as the other.

Luke 6:19

And the whole multitude sought to touch Him, for power went out from Him and healed them all.

Luke 7:21

And that very hour He cured many of infirmities, afflictions, and evil spirits; and to many blind He gave sight.

Luke 8:43–48

Now a woman, having a flow of blood for twelve years, who had spent all her livelihood on physicians and could not be healed by any, came from behind and touched the border of His garment. And immediately her flow of blood stopped. And Jesus said, "Who touched Me?" When all denied it, Peter and those with him said, "Master, the multitudes throng and press You, and You say, 'Who touched Me?'" But Jesus said, "Somebody touched Me, for I perceived power going out from Me." Now when the woman saw that she was not hidden, she came trembling; and falling down before Him, she declared to Him in the presence of all the people the reason she had touched Him and how she was healed immediately. And He said to her, "Daughter, be of good cheer; your faith has made you well. Go in peace."

Luke 14:1-6

> *Now it happened, as He went into the house of one of the rulers of the Pharisees to eat bread on the Sabbath, that they watched Him closely. And behold, there was a certain man before Him who had dropsy. And Jesus, answering, spoke to the lawyers and Pharisees, saying, "Is it lawful to heal on the Sabbath?"*

> *But they kept silent. And He took him and healed him, and let him go. Then He answered them, saying, "Which of you, having a donkey or an ox that has fallen into a pit, will not immediately pull him out on the Sabbath day?" And they could not answer Him regarding these things.*

Luke 22:49-51

> *When those around Him saw what was going to happen, they said to Him, "Lord, shall we strike with the sword?" And one of them struck the servant of the high priest and cut off his right ear. But Jesus answered and said, "Permit even this." And He touched his ear and healed him.*

John 5:6-9

> *When Jesus saw him lying there, and knew that he already had been in that condition a long time, He said to him, "Do you want to be made well?" The sick man answered Him, "Sir, I have no man to put*

me into the pool when the water is stirred up; but while I am coming, another steps down before me." Jesus said to him, "Rise, take up your bed and walk." And immediately the man was made well, took up his bed, and walked. And that day was the Sabbath.

Acts 3:6-8

Then Peter said, "Silver and gold I do not have, but what I do have I give you: In the name of Jesus Christ of Nazareth, rise up and walk." And he took him by the right hand and lifted him up, and immediately his feet and ankle bones received strength. So he, leaping up, stood and walked and entered the temple with them—walking, leaping, and praising God.

Acts 3:16

And His name, through faith in His name, has made this man strong, whom you see and know. Yes, the faith which comes through Him has given him this perfect soundness in the presence of you all.

Acts 5:12

And through the hands of the apostles many signs and wonders were done among the people. And they were all with one accord in Solomon's Porch.

Acts 10:38

How God anointed Jesus of Nazareth with the Holy Spirit and with power, who went about doing good and healing all who were oppressed by the devil, for God was with Him.

Romans 8:35–39

Who shall separate us from the love of Christ? Shall tribulation, or distress, or persecution, or famine, or nakedness, or peril, or sword? As it is written: "For Your sake we are killed all day long; we are accounted as sheep for the slaughter."

Yet in all these things we are more than conquerors through Him who loved us. For I am persuaded that neither death nor life, nor angels nor principalities nor powers, nor things present nor things to come, nor height nor depth, nor any other created thing, shall be able to separate us from the love of God which is in Christ Jesus our Lord.

Philippians 4:6–7

Be anxious for nothing, but in everything by prayer and supplication, with thanksgiving, let your requests be made known to God; and the peace of God, which surpasses all understanding, will guard your hearts and minds through Christ Jesus.

First Peter 2:24

Who Himself bore our sins in His own body on the tree, that we, having died to sins, might live for righteousness—by whose stripes you were healed.

James 5:13-16

Is anyone among you suffering? Let him pray. Is anyone cheerful? Let him sing psalms. Is anyone among you sick? Let him call for the elders of the church, and let them pray over him, anointing him with oil in the name of the Lord. And the prayer of faith will save the sick, and the Lord will raise him up. And if he has committed sins, he will be forgiven. Confess your trespasses to one another, and pray for one another, that you may be healed. The effective, fervent prayer of a righteous man avails much.

Third John 1:2

Beloved, I pray that you may prosper in all things and be in health, just as your soul prospers.

Revelation 22:1-2

And he showed me a pure river of water of life, clear as crystal, proceeding from the throne of God and of the Lamb. In the middle of its street, and on either side of the river, was the tree of life, which bore twelve fruits, each tree yielding its fruit every month. The leaves of the tree were for the healing of the nations.

Second Kings 4:8–37:
A Double Miracle for the Shunammite Woman

Now it happened one day that Elisha went to Shunem, where there was a notable woman, and she persuaded him to eat some food. So it was, as often as he passed by, he would turn in there to eat some food. And she said to her husband, "Look now, I know that this is a holy man of God, who passes by us regularly. Please, let us make a small upper room on the wall; and let us put a bed for him there, and a table and a chair and a lampstand; so it will be, whenever he comes to us, he can turn in there."

And it happened one day that he came there, and he turned in to the upper room and lay down there. Then he said to Gehazi his servant, "Call this Shunammite woman." When he had called her, she stood before him. And he said to him, "Say now to her, 'Look, you have been concerned for us with all this care. What can I do for you? Do you want me to speak on your behalf to the king or to the commander of the army?'"

She answered, "I dwell among my own people."

So he said, "What then is to be done for her?"

And Gehazi answered, "Actually, she has no son, and her husband is old."

So he said, "Call her." When he had called her, she stood in the doorway. Then he said, "About this time next year you shall embrace a son."

And she said, "No, my lord. Man of God, do not lie to your maidservant!"

But the woman conceived, and bore a son when the appointed time had come, of which Elisha had told her. And the child grew. Now it happened one day that he went out to his father, to the reapers. And he said to his father, "My head, my head!"

So he said to a servant, "Carry him to his mother." When he had taken him and brought him to his mother, he sat on her knees till noon, and then died. And she went up and laid him on the bed of the man of God, shut the door upon him, and went out. Then she called to her husband, and said, "Please send me one of the young men and one of the donkeys, that I may run to the man of God and come back."

So he said, "Why are you going to him today? It is neither the New Moon nor the Sabbath."

And she said, "It is well." Then she saddled a donkey, and said to her servant, "Drive, and go forward; do not slacken the pace for me unless I tell you." And so she departed, and went to the man of God at Mount Carmel.

So it was, when the man of God saw her afar off, that he said to his servant Gehazi, "Look, the Shunammite woman! Please run now to meet her, and say to her, 'Is it well with you? Is it well with your husband? Is it well with the child?'"

And she answered, "It is well." Now when she came to the man of God at the hill, she caught him by the feet, but Gehazi came near to push her away. But the man of God said, "Let her alone; for her soul is in deep distress, and the LORD has hidden it from me, and has not told me."

So she said, "Did I ask a son of my lord? Did I not say, 'Do not deceive me'?"

Then he said to Gehazi, "Get yourself ready, and take my staff in your hand, and be on your way. If you meet anyone, do not greet him; and if anyone greets you, do not answer him; but lay my staff on the face of the child."

And the mother of the child said, "As the LORD lives, and as your soul lives, I will not leave you."

So he arose and followed her. Now Gehazi went on ahead of them, and laid the staff on the face of the child; but there was neither voice nor hearing. Therefore he went back to meet him, and told him, saying, "The child has not awakened."

When Elisha came into the house, there was the child, lying dead on his bed. He went in therefore, shut the door behind the two of them, and prayed to the LORD. And he went up and lay on the child, and put his mouth on his mouth, his eyes on his eyes, and his hands on his hands; and he stretched himself out on the child, and the flesh of the child became warm. He returned and walked back and forth in the house, and again went up and stretched himself out on him; then the child sneezed seven times, and the child opened his eyes. And he called Gehazi and said, "Call this Shunammite woman." So he called her. And when she came in to him, he said, "Pick up your son." So she went in, fell at his feet, and bowed to the ground; then she picked up her son and went out.

Second Kings 5:1-14: Naaman, the Syrian Leper, Healed

Now Naaman, commander of the army of the king of Syria, was a great and honorable man in the eyes of his master, because by him the LORD had given victory to Syria. He was also a mighty man of valor, but a leper. And the Syrians had gone out on raids, and had brought back captive a young girl from the land of Israel. She waited on Naaman's wife. Then she said to her mistress, "If only my master were with the prophet who is in Samaria! For he would heal him of his leprosy." And Naaman went in and told his master, saying, "Thus and thus said the girl who is from the land of Israel."

Then the king of Syria said, "Go now, and I will send a letter to the king of Israel." So he departed and took with him ten talents of silver, six thousand shekels of gold, and ten changes of clothing. Then he brought the letter to the king of Israel, which said,

Now be advised, when this letter comes to you, that I have sent Naaman my servant to you, that you may heal him of his leprosy.

And it happened, when the king of Israel read the letter, that he tore his clothes and said, "Am I God, to kill and make alive, that this man sends a man to me to heal him of his leprosy? Therefore please consider, and see how he seeks a quarrel with me."

So it was, when Elisha the man of God heard that the king of Israel had torn his clothes, that he sent to the king, saying, "Why have you torn your clothes? Please let him come to me, and he shall know that there is a prophet in Israel."

Then Naaman went with his horses and chariot, and he stood at the door of Elisha's house. And Elisha sent a messenger to him, saying, "Go and wash in the Jordan seven times, and your flesh shall be restored to you, and you shall be clean." But Naaman became furious, and went away and said, "Indeed, I said to myself, 'He will surely come out to me, and stand and call on the name of the LORD his God, and wave his hand over the place, and heal the leprosy.' Are not the Abanah and the Pharpar, the rivers of Damascus, better than all the waters of Israel? Could I not wash in them and be clean?" So he turned and went away in a rage. And his servants came near and spoke to him, and said, "My father, if the prophet had told you to do something great, would you not have done it? How much more then, when he says to you, 'Wash, and be clean'?" So he went down and dipped seven times in the Jordan, according to the saying of the man of God; and his flesh was restored like the flesh of a little child, and he was clean.

Bibliography

James Strong, *The New Strong's Exhaustive Concordance of the Bible*, "Hebrew and Aramaic Dictionary," (Nashville, TN: Thomas Nelson Publishers, 1996).

James Strong, *The New Strong's Exhaustive Concordance of the Bible*, "Greek Dictionary," (Nashville, TN: Thomas Nelson Publishers, 1996).

About the Author

At the tender age of 15, Pastor Kynan committed his life to Jesus Christ and was subsequently filled with the Holy Spirit. After getting involved in his local church, God made His call manifest to Kynan audibly. For many years, Kynan served in the local church and was involved with various ministries. After running from the call of God; he was finally arrested by the Holy Spirit. Several years ago, the Lord told Kynan to begin a teaching ministry in Tampa, FL. At this point, the vision for Grace & Peace Global Fellowship was birthed.

> *For if by one man's offense death reigned by one; much more they which receive abundance of grace and of the gift of righteousness shall reign in life by one, Jesus Christ* (Romans 5:17).

This is the vision and mission of our ministry: to see the person, power, and presence of Jesus Christ manifested in the lives of people everywhere that they might reign in life. Through this ministry we desire to see millions of souls saved and restored through the Gospel of Jesus Christ. We accomplish this mission by proclaiming the unadulterated, life-changing, Word of God. Our outreach ministry serves as the catalyst to spread this message. Every week we provide resources to people so that they might become more conscious of Christ's love for them and enter into the fullness of His finished work and thereby be positioned to walk in their God ordained assignment, namely the Great Commissioned as outlined in Matthew 28:19.

Our weekly podcast (FaithTalk) serves as a platform to discuss various issues in the body of Christ and the world, and shed light on those issues through the illumination of God's Word. We are committed to spreading the gospel through our preaching ministry, speaking engagements, teaching resources, and internet and media platforms.

To date, we have reached countless numbers of people with the gospel. Through the combined efforts of our weekly outreach ministry and new media resources we have exposed thousands to the Gospel of Grace every single week. Currently we are communicating God's Word to people in North America, India, Haiti, and Nigeria. We are engaging in several outreach efforts, which have a global impact.

Pastor Kynan is committed to allowing the power and anointing of the Holy Spirit to flow through him and touch God's people. He is a committed husband, mentor, and father to three beautiful children: Ella, Naomi, and Isaac.

For information on booking, requesting prayer, or supporting this ministry write to:

Kynan Bridges Ministries

P.O BOX 159

Ruskin, FL 33575

1.800.516.7038

Or visit us at: www.kynanbridges.org

IN THE RIGHT HANDS, THIS BOOK WILL CHANGE LIVES!

Most of the people who need this message will not be looking for this book. To change their lives, you need to put a copy of this book in their hands.

> *But others (seeds) fell into good ground, and brought forth fruit, some a hundred-fold, some sixty-fold, some thirty-fold* (Matthew 13:8).

Our ministry is constantly seeking methods to find the good ground, the people who need this anointed message to change their lives. Will you help us reach these people?

> *Remember this—a farmer who plants only a few seeds will get a small crop. But the one who plants generously will get a generous crop* (2 Corinthians 9:6).

EXTEND THIS MINISTRY BY SOWING
3 BOOKS, 5 BOOKS, 10 BOOKS, OR MORE TODAY,
AND BECOME A LIFE CHANGER!

Thank you,

[signature]

Don Nori Sr., Founder
Destiny Image
Since 1982

shelby simpson spencer

J
E
S
U
S

CYA THEN